CONCRETE LIFEGUARDS

Steven Christopher Bialek

In loving memory of Jeanne L. Dugan.

Dedicated to all the men and women
of the emergency medical services who
have and are still saving lives.

CONTENTS

PROLOGUE

I don't think I'm alone to have a bag full of memories after a professional career. You know, the bag, or folder, or box where you throw the events you can't quite process at the time. Like most, I have my share of blessings, joys, and nightmares stored there.

Quite often, before I open it, I sigh deeply. Looking back at the events that unfolded, I find myself reminiscing. *Even if we all sat down and picked through each other's minds for infinity, it would be hard to figure out the reasoning behind the destruction caused to so many lives. Perhaps it was ignorance? Maybe malice? How about indifference?* Most people, I included, would love to think that we can turn back the hands of time. Alas, they have yet to invent the time machine.

Inside my bag, there are close to thirty-five years of history. Every piece of paper and scribbled note reminds me that I have been fortunate and blessed to work with a most talented (and strange) bunch of coworkers, many of whom perished during the events of 9/11/2001.

I've looked a little more closely at the big picture, and as cliché as it sounds, I find myself looking for answers that only God knows. In retrospect, I think on that fateful day, the Fire Department Chaplain was taken first so he could greet all those who died. Whether we're members of the services or civilians, we are all still brothers and sisters in God's eyes. We all came into this world naked, and by God, we shall stand before him naked on judgment day.

CHAPTER ONE

How it all began

The year is 1983. The exact date escapes me now. However, twenty-two-year-old Steven was driving a school bus. One of my co-workers, a retired city employee—a former transit police officer, I think—asked what I was going to do with the rest of my life. Just as an ambulance passed the on the street where we were parked. I really didn't know what to tell him. But deep inside, I knew I had to come up with something.

Subconsciously I have always wanted to help others. I could point to several events that happened during my childhood, but one sticks out. In the '70s, when I was about seventeen years old, I used to work in a newspaper stand in the corner of Lexington and 42nd Street. For those who aren't familiar with that intersection, 42 street is a two-way street east to west, and Lexington is a one-way street that goes south. A car was turning from forty-second street onto Lexington. Another was going straight on 42nd Street.

Meanwhile a woman was crossing the street. I can't say for sure where the misunderstanding between the drivers was, but they collided, trapping the pedestrian in the process. Along with other people, I ran toward the accident to see what was going on. Thinking I could help, I approached the wreckage and moved some debris out of the way, but nearby people pulled me away. *It's dangerous.* Mere minutes later, an ambulance rushed in. The first responders worked tirelessly to help her. And yeah, one more thing, the sight wasn't so pretty, but it didn't bother me as much as I thought it was going to.

I still think about that day.

Anyway, so it was that the retired cop lent me five hundred dollars so I could go to school to get certified as an emergency medical technician. Because at the time I was working as a sports counselor as well as a bus driver for Champions Sports Club headquartered in Manhattan, I went to night school in Saint Barnabas hospital three times a week; Monday, Wednesday, and Thursday, 7-9 p.m. I did that for six months.

A day after the certification paper came in the mail, I went to the Associated Ambulance-private company in Flushing, Queens. I presented them with the certification. They hired me.

I worked for the private sector until 1988, but deep down, I knew I had to apply and join the civil servants of New York. So, I filled out all possible applications and sent them out.

You may call it fate, chance, or even destiny that the New York City Emergency Medical Technician application replied first. By this time of my life, I was reaching the dreaded thirty years old. That was, and I believe still is, the average cutoff age to become a civil servant. I would've joined the first one to reply. Emergency Medical Services returned first, and after an extensive two-year wait period, off I went.

***

As my career was moving along, my personal life was changing as well. I met Darlene in Long Island sometime in the late eighties. Back then, she was a nurse's aide, and, as my benevolent had helped me, I helped her with the civil servant exams. At first, she was a loving person. She wished to have a house and kids out in Long Island, the suburbs, which was typical at the time. The only problem was she wanted it yesterday, and since it wasn't foreseen in the near future, the relationship and later marriage, didn't look good for either of us. Because she was a Police Officer, logic dictated the slight possibility that guns could be involved if the marriage in that state would drag for much longer. About five years later, we went our separate ways.

Because the assignments were visually and mentally disturbing, at the end of the workday, I would sit down and write whatever I experienced. Recreating them from my memory. That was my coping mechanism.

But I digress.

After I paid my benevolent back at a rate of $50 a week, I began the academy.

Located in Fort Totten, in Queens, the New York City Emergency Medical Services Academy was a strange beast all of its own. There were ducks everywhere, soldiers with M-16's, cars, trucks. To top this off, a grumpy four-star general, the fort's commander, had strict orders. "Anyone who hits these poultry beasts with a motor vehicle shall be brought in front of a military tribunal to face charges of killing an endangered species!"

What is going on around here?

"Come on, Rocky." My classmates would reply. "Be thankful we can drive on a military base. Did you see how long it would take to walk to the academy from the parking lot? It's at least two beers away!" Back then, we measured time in how long it would take to drink a twelve-ounce can of beer; each beer took us about five minutes. Hence, it was a ten-minute walk.

For the next eight weeks, I trained to work with the emergency medical services for New York. The minimal passing grade was seventy-five. If I failed three exams and my average fell below the minimum, I would flunk out of the academy. But I didn't.

The only thing I recall from graduation day is being glad it was over. I've always hated school and uniforms; this was no different. After twelve years of parochial school—you know, blue pants, white shirt, clip-on tie, black shoes—I realized God had played a cruel trick on me. It looked like that for the next twenty-five years, I was going to have to wear a uniform again. The only difference was the color of the pants was puke green!

It wasn't so bad once I realized I was getting paid to wear the uniform this time around.

From what I remember, the ceremony was lovely. My family showed up, the class Valedictorian, Chiefs, and whatnot gave a few speeches. Catered cold cuts and sodas were included. It was capped off with being presented with a certificate of completion for the EMS Academy by the Deputy Chief of the Emergency Medical Services department.

Out of fifty-five trainees, only forty-four graduated. A total of eight written exams and hands-on practicals had nearly been enough to bring on an ulcer. I remember that a few instructors had strange ways of treating patients. However, mostly it was by the book. Little did I know that when I hit the streets eight weeks later, the book had to be thrown out, and a new set of rules had to be implemented.

I was taught the fine art of improvisational life-saving techniques, which changed on a per-call basis. It included utilizing anything or anyone around me to stabilize that patient. Save a life.

***

Let me be a little realistic here and say something I think we can all agree upon. No matter how eventful one's career is, we aren't doing something heroic or worth mentioning every day 24/7. I would estimate that a good percentage of the 911 calls which came in were, what I used to call, sick jobs: *I've got a cold, take me to the hospital cause I have no car,* or *I have a doctor's appointment at the clinic, and I don't want to wait in the emergency room.* I believe that this thinking reasons that the doctor will get to you faster by calling an ambulance. It's a misconception. Nothing guarantees that someone will be seen more quickly if they arrive with an ambulance for a cold. In fact, it's sad to think that, at times, I couldn't respond to something a lot more severe because of these sick calls. Something like a respiratory-arrest job secondary to asthma. I would hear those calls and sigh. Sigh because the ambulance I was driving was carrying someone with a slightly high fever.

Having explained the above, I still want to stress that I can't remember all the times I used my skills to help save a life. They were numerous. But to this day, I can remember all those poor souls who died in my arms. If I could have gotten there a little sooner, would it have made the difference between life and death?

***

The life of a civil servant is filled with questions, dilemmas, and the occasional self-doubting moments. Just like everyone else, I would mostly talk about the jobs with my peers. Occasionally I would talk to others, like that doctor who pronounced the two-year-old. I even asked a priest, while I was drunk, I should add, if I was doing the right thing,

"Look, I've got five months of medical training, and they're sending me on assignments a cardiologist wouldn't touch because his malpractice insurance might go up!" The universal answer from all support groups would be, "You can't save the world; you can only do what you are trained to do."

I can save the world, and *I want to make a difference* were my guiding stars when I came out of the academy. I still sigh when I think of those times. It took me about five or six years to realize that there is only one me and six million potential patients out there. I wish I could split myself into pieces to save them all. Like the priest told me, the best I can do is to save one at a time.

Sadly, some of my coworkers are no longer with us because they overdosed and died; they basically did themselves in. That became a real problem in the mid-nineties. Alcohol was part of my daily life as well. It was a habit caused by the combination of a wife "who wanted everything yesterday" and my job. Unfortunately, I could not meet her demands and balance what was going on at home and at work simultaneously. But it's too early to talk about that at this point.

I don't wish to relive each and every case because they suck and still give me nightmares. I remember that most of them have lousy endings (I can never remember the happy ending ones), where either the patient died on the way to the hospital or the patient got locked up by the police.

CHAPTER TWO

My roller coaster ride starts

After graduation in 1991, I was told to report to EMS Station 45 for my assignment. I was briefed by the station's Deputy Chief and introduced to the fantastic people I was going to work with. I was told I was free to go and to report for work at fourteen-hundred hours on July 4th, 1991, the following day.

To say that Station 45 needed a little work was an understatement. The inside was pretty sad once you got a good look at it in the light. The paint job looked like it had been done forty years ago, and it probably was. The light blue paint on the cement wall was peeling off. Everything in that station was totally outdated. The old rotary phones affixed on the wall by the entrance corridor weren't connected, but, holy hell, as soon as I walked in for the first time, I thought that place belonged in a museum. The skylight in the middle of the station proved somewhat of a relief to the eyesores around the room. I think that was because it allowed me to see outside, not inside the building. Later I realized that to complete the image, the morgue was next door.

Well, it's not a freaking five-star hotel, but at least it's close to home. Like most things in life, I got used to the place.

Every six months or so, we would get new furniture from the crews that worked the wealthy neighborhoods. They salvaged whatever was appropriate and necessary for the station. Once in a while, we had a nice secondhand couch or a ripped La-Z-Boy recliner. No matter how bad the color was, it definitely made the place more livable.

I was a little perplexed with the station's furniture arrangement at first. That was, until the first rain of the season rolled in. It became evident that we had a leaky skylight; buckets popped up all over the station, and the furniture was shifted to strange locations. It was then when I understood that the inside layout depended on how bad the forecast was for the week.

Once computers came in, the chance of electrocution was far too great for the city not to take notice. It was then decided that the skylight should be fixed, not for the sake of the employees, but for the computers.

The file cabinets, desks, and chairs that the supervisors used in a separate office were in just about the same condition as the paint job. There were at least two instances of employees being taken to the hospital with neck and back injuries because the chairs were utterly broken. After a while, it turned into a cruel game of musical chairs, until finally the captain threw them all out and bought some new ones.

The new seating arrangements were applied with a bit of fanfare. It took a while for us to get used to an actual chair that worked. Most of us instinctively braced ourselves when sitting in anyone's chair anyway. It became a habit. Family members and friends who didn't work with us and weren't aware of our chair situation would watch when we sat down and notice how we braced for a fall. It got to the point where people would check their own chairs after we left, wondering if the chair we sat in, was broken.

The bathroom wall was like the local newspaper; even the chiefs would come to read its contents to find out what was going on in their division. It was funny because the leaders didn't think we'd caught on to their little "I know what is going on in my division" game.

We knew that they knew; the bathroom wall gave them the scoop.

Every week we made up a new topic: usually, who was screwing who or messed up on a particular job.

In other stations, employees would pass out after shooting heroin. That didn't mean they were bad people, as long as they showed up for work. We all had our faults; it was all about controlling those personal demons.

The supervisor's office and supply rooms were in trailers, supported by cement blocks. It was surreal to have a trailer be called the Chief's office. Even more surreal to sit in one of those for a command discipline hearing, or as we called it, "Kangaroo Court." We all knew that the trailer could collapse at any time, or at the least tip over if someone outside kicked out a few cinder blocks. Considering some of the penalties which were handed down, that was a strong possibility.

The chief assigned to head Station 45 in the '90s was fair. At least that was the general consensus. Even though we knew that he read the bathroom wall rumors, he ran the station with a "please don't screw up" attitude. And when someone inevitably did, depending on how he looked at that current screw-up, he would either file it in his desk in the "I'll get to it when Hell freezes over" drawer. Or would issue a transfer order to a foot post on the Goethals Bridge. The main thing was that he was well-liked by everybody in the station, which was rare, especially for a chief in our line of work.

As with most higher-level supervisors, our Chief was a lieutenant before he got the promotion. Years prior, he told me about a true story that happened to him when he worked in Manhattan. In the late seventies, a crane collapsed at 68th Street and 3rd Avenue and pinned a woman for twelve hours. While this lady was pinned under a (god knows how many tons) crane, he crawled underneath it and held this poor woman's hand while others tried so desperately to get the crane off her lower extremities. Eventually, it was lifted off her by a pair of cranes from the local power and electric company. He received a medal. She thanked him, and he never forgot that.

He told me that some ten years later, after another crane collapsed in Queens. I was assigned to the job, along with the chief, only this time, the patient wasn't so lucky. As a matter of fact, the patient was dead before he hit the ground. His back had snapped on the way down. By the time he arrived on-site, we were walking back from the place where it happened. There was debris and destruction everywhere.

"Mister Bialek, I never regretted what I did that day," the chief said, referring to his first experience. "But I'll be damned if I ever see one of you do the same foolish thing I did." Then he added, "Without letting me know."

He then proceeded to his command car and asked for the medical examiner to expedite because removal would have to be done ASAP due to the crowd of onlookers.

CHAPTER THREE

Randy's short straw

My first partner, Randy, was a veteran of EMS for over ten years. He was a short, nervous Italian fellow in his mid-thirties with two kids and a house out in the suburbs. He was as nice a guy as you would want to teach you the ropes of this profession. Not only did he have the patience for dealing with emotionally disturbed patients (he also ended up one), but his driving skills were most excellent. Especially driving to 911 calls for patients having a cardiac arrest.

At first, I was a little nervous. And after about

three weeks of being the Medic/EMT and him as a driver, I figured that even with all the lights and sirens we had on the ambulance, the likelihood of us getting hurt was above what I called normal.

Considering the chances we took running red lights when we were basically driving like mad racecar drivers, I think it's safe to say we had a legion of Guardian Angels riding along with us. In crash helmets!

***

When the fires were burning down the old, dilapidated houses of South Jamaica in the late nineties, a 911 call was assigned to one of our units for a 10-75, an all-hands fire of a three-story wooden house. Randy was working, but I was off.

The structure was fully engulfed in flames in a few hours, and all the firefighters were scrambling to manage it. The Emergency Medical Unit was standing outside, watching. They were preparing to treat potential injuries of firefighters working on this job. Then the unit got word of possible civilian fatalities on the second floor. One of the EMTs was going to be escorted by the firefighters to the second floor to pronounce the victims.

Evidently, Randy drew the short straw.

From what I read in the newspapers, an elderly grandfather took his grandkids upstairs once he saw the flames on the ground floor. He proceeded to the bathroom and filled the tub up with water, grabbed a mattress from one of the bedrooms, and pulled it over the cast iron tub with him and his grandsons submerged while the flames were raging downstairs.

The following day, Randy came back a changed man. I asked him what happened a few times. "People soup" is what still remains with me from his answer. After that job, Randy became less focused on what he was doing; he seemed almost in a daze.

Most of us working had issues of sorts, so he fit right in. I felt terrible a few years later when I realized I'd neglected to notice my own partner's cry for help as the jobs became more frequent and visually disturbing. After a few months, Randy took it upon himself to call 911 while in a patient's house and holding a knife on himself, threatening suicide after swallowing the patient's pills.

Once a supervisor showed up, and after a tense thirty minutes of negotiation, Randy agreed to go to the hospital in the lieutenant's vehicle. At the same time, another unit took the original patient to the hospital.

While on the way to the hospital, Randy attempted

to jump out of the command car—twice. The first time was aborted thanks to the lieutenant's fast actions. The second time—let's just say Randy was determined—he exited the vehicle by jumping out at approximately thirty miles per hour on Grand Central Parkway. He then proceeded to run against traffic, causing a *slight* problem with on-coming cars.

It wasn't until John Gleason, who by random chance happened to be driving another EMS unit on the other side, approached the same exit. He basically saved Randy's life by tackling him out of the fast lane and physically dragging him off the highway.

After a few months of seeing a psychiatrist, Randy was put back to work!

One year later, I was told he was handling the phones at headquarters. When he relapsed, the City of New York decided his services were no longer needed. He applied for social security, and it was granted to him.

After that, I would call Randy's house once a year during the holidays and wish him well. But after two or three years, he just stopped answering the phone. I found out later that Randy had a mental breakdown, possibly since one of those children Randy pronounced in the house fire was the same age as Randy's eight-year-old. Perhaps he reminded him of his child.

It's hard to say what made Randy do what he did, but I'll tell you one thing: no matter how you look at it, this job contributed to his mental breakdown.

***

I didn't have any children at the time, so I could only sympathize and try to put myself in Randy's proverbial shoes. But my life and career events continued unfolding.

Sometime around 1996 and '97, because of a high volume of 911 calls, our unit was sent to cover another area of Queens. Because of Randy's meltdown on Grand Central Parkway, I was working with Bobby, a fellow EMT who worked on the same shift. It was then when he realized what my nickname, Rocky, meant.

"Rocky," Bobby mused as we drove down the boulevard. "How'd you get the name?"

"What name?" I answered, sitting in the passenger seat scribbling our last assignment down in the logbook.

"Rocky." Bobby laughed. "You don't look like Rocky, and I'm sure you never looked like him either."

I realized what he was talking about. "Oh, the nickname. Well, I was a bike messenger in the mid-seventies for Mr. Messenger. The owner called me 'Rocky' after a cartoon character."

"What?" Bobby seemed a little confused.

"Rocky, the movie, wasn't even out yet. Remember Bullwinkle J. Moose?" I asked.

"Yeah." Bobby was starting to see where I was going.

"The boss named me after Bullwinkle's sidekick in the cartoon show, Rocky the flying squirrel."

Bobby gave me that puzzled look.

"Because I was so fast on the bike, like Rocky the flying squirrel, get it?" I said, laughing. "I guess the name stuck, and then the movie with Sylvester Stallone came out a year later, and the rest is history."

"So, your nickname is after a cartoon character?" Bobby looked at me over his shoulder.

"Yep."

"That explanation wasn't very melodramatic at all." Bobby laughed. "I feel cheated."

"How do you think I felt when somebody would introduce me to some girl and say, 'this is my buddy Rocky,'" I said. "You could see the disappointment on the girl's face once they saw me. Like you said, I never really looked like Sylvester Stallone!"

We both chuckled.

"Four-Two-Charlie for an assignment," Queens Central dispatcher voice reverberated through the ambulance's speakers.

"Bingo." Bobby picked up the microphone, acknowledging the dispatcher. "Send it over, Central."

I peeked at the computer screen. The job information on the patient sounded straightforward; it fit the description of a sick job. Not really life-threatening for the patient, or so we both thought, and best of all, it was only a few blocks away from Flushing Hospital.

The area was full of typical two-family brownstone houses with small lawns as front yards, surrounded by shallow fences. A mature lady around fifty answered the door and escorted us to her husband, who was in the living room.

The first thing that struck me was the patient's color. It was way off. He looked grey, which is not a good color to be.

I asked Bobby to get whatever information he could from the patient's wife. I sat down in front of the patient with my equipment. After introducing myself to the gentleman, I asked him his name, how old he was, and if anything hurt. He said he didn't feel right, general malaise type of thing, and the patient told me he was fifty-five years old.

My god, he looks 70.

I told him I would take his blood pressure and pulse; the patient didn't object. So, I began to take his blood pressure, and...there was none.

Hmm, let me try it again.

I did it three times! Still nothing.

I can't find a freaking pulse either. I began shuffling my equipment.

"Is everything okay?" The patient noticed that I looked a little perplexed.

"Sure, sure, everything is fine." I reached for the portable oxygen tank we usually bring with us. Maybe the oxygen will get his color back a little. I've seen dead people look better than this guy. I pulled the mask out and slid it over his head.

"Stay here for a moment; I'll be right back." I walked over to Bobby and gestured to him that I wanted to talk. Excusing himself, he walked over to where I was.

"What's up?"

"I think our patient is dead and still talking to me."

"Say what?" Bobby looked me in the eye.

"I took his blood pressure and pulse three times. I can't get a read on him. You try. Maybe it's me." It was general practice to have your partner try a procedure if something was not right.

"Well, the guy is definitely not dead; he doesn't look a hundred percent, but he's not dead."

"He is far from a hundred percent. You find a pulse."

Bobby took out his own stethoscope and the blood pressure cuff I was holding and walked over to the patient.

"Is everything okay?" our patient asked once again, noticing the shuffle.

"Everything is fine. You look great," Bobby replied.

His wife told me that her husband, our patient, hadn't been feeling well all day; that's why she called 911.

About a minute later, while listening to the patient's wife tell me all the medication her husband was taking, I recognized Bobby's voice on my portable radio. He was giving a notification for our patient to Flushing Hospital and ruling a tentative diagnosis of a Descending Aortic Aneurism. Bobby also requested the hospital have a surgeon on standby. "Our ETA to the hospital is seven minutes."

Bobby calmly walked over to me. "I got a blood pressure reading and a pulse on the other arm; it's really low, but he's got one. The first arm still nothing. The patient is complaining of a tearing sensation in his lower back. It's a telltale sign of an aortic aneurism."

I swallowed. "I absolutely blanked out on that one."

"We have about five minutes before this guy craps out on us," Bobby whispered.

"Great," I sarcastically whispered back. I feared that the patient would collapse and drop dead in front of his wife once we moved him.

We got him on a stair chair and carried him outside into the ambulance, then transferred him from the stair chair to the stretcher like he was a bottle of nitroglycerin with the cap off. We were at the hospital in about seven minutes, where a trauma team and surgeon were waiting for us in the receiving bay. Bobby got out of the driver's side and briefed the M.D. on what was going on. Before we knew it, the guy was whisked away and upstairs into the O.R. on our stretcher.

About twenty minutes later, an orderly brought our stretcher back and told us the doctor told him to say, "Good job."

"Tell him." I pointed to Bobby.

"I guess he's still alive," I said to Bobby as we took our stretcher and left the hospital.

"Apparently." Bobby sighed. "I wonder if he is going to make it."

No one told us if that patient made it or not, but at least he was breathing last we saw him. Though this assignment sounded routine, it wasn't.

***

The dispatchers that I knew in the Communications Division had to be the best in the whole world. These guys didn't freak out when personnel screamed for help, or a cardiac arrest was imminent in their sector, and they had no units to send. Somehow, they found resources. Even though the city of New York spent millions to put a computer system in to help them make efficient decisions, I don't think it worked as well as they thought it did.

The wall in front of them consisted of a giant checkerboard. Each square, called a sector, represented twenty blocks across and twenty blocks down. When a 911 call came in for a Motor Vehicle Accident in a corner square of the checkerboard, the ambulance covering that square should be assigned. However, chances were that the ambulance was already dispatched for a sick job or a bogus 911 call, so the dispatcher would try and get the closest ambulance covering the next square.

If that ambulance square was busy, they tried the next, and the next, until they found a unit that could respond in ten minutes or less. This was where the computer was supposed to come in handy. But like always, things didn't go according to the script. "Improvising direction" had to be done by the dispatcher in the Hot Seat.

Eventually, an ambulance would be assigned, depending on whether there was a full moon out or not. For some reason, during those times, calls would double. Unfortunately, we didn't magically have twice as many ambulances to dispatch.

Average greetings with the dispatcher would go a little bit like this. I would test my radio by transmitting at the beginning of my tour. "Four-Two-Charles for a radio check, please."

He would follow with a "five by five" in a monotone voice. His vocal sounds had a soothing, familiar effect on all of us. "Are you in the show?"

"Yep," I would respond.

CHAPTER FOUR

The Pin-Job, 1993

"I have a trauma job, car vs. tree with numerous injuries, location Belt Parkway, looks real, we have numerous 911 calls coming in," the dispatcher explained the assignment that was displayed in our ambulance's computer screen.

"Four-Two-Charles on its way."

"Give me a preliminary when you get there," Mark, the dispatcher, said.

I never noticed back then how impressive the Throgs Neck Bridge, which connects the boroughs of the Bronx and Queens, looked during a sparsely clouded night. Driving an ambulance with its strobes and red flashing lights on could be pretty breathtaking, yes, even for the ones who were inside, operating it. Especially the way the colored lights reflected off the archway, suspension cables, and the spotlights fastened to the bridge.

As I drove on the bridge, the full moon peeked through the clouds and shone its light through the massive steel structure. All sorts of large and small vehicles sped on it. One hoped the individuals and passenger cars would arrive safely at their intended destinations. As we knew all too well, roads could be dangerous and unforgiving at any given time, depending on who the vehicle operator was, especially on a rainy night when the ambulance radio interrupted the scenery.

"Four-Two Charlie, what's your location?"

"Right now, we're on the Clearview Expressway heading east," I replied.

"Did you get the new location on your data terminal?"

"Ten-Four Central, I did get that new location." I paused for a second, then got back on the air. "So

Central…exactly how many locations do you have for this Motor vehicle Accident?"

"That would be about five or six, Charlie," Mark replied, "all of them in the same general vicinity. Looks real. Just give me a confirmation once you're on the scene. I have five other units checking the other locations."

Before I could put the microphone down, I glanced over to Owen, who was putting his heavy-duty plastic surgical gloves on.

"You are planning on doing some actual work tonight?"

Owen just looked at me, then swung his head toward the front and side window to anticipate any sign of the trouble that might come. Owen had a sixth sense; once I saw him put gloves on, it made me nervous cause every time he put them on, I had nightmares for the next few weeks.

We pulled the ambulance over on the shoulder of a grassy section of the Cross-Island Parkway about four minutes later. I picked up the radio's microphone.

"Ah, Central, I think we got the location Cross Island Parkway and Linden, right across from the racetrack. I'll give you a twenty in a minute."

At this time, all that I was taught in the EMS/FDNY Academy was shoved entirely out the back door, into a ditch, and buried. We were initially trained to do that ten-second survey at a significant multiple casualty incident (MCI). Well…to be honest, we didn't have ten seconds this time.

A female police officer ran up to us. She gave us some information, and with a huff and a puff, put down a spent fire extinguisher and sat on the grass to catch her breath. Getting out of the ambulance, I saw a car wrapped around a massive tree. The front of the vehicle was smoldering. A deafening, continuous scream was coming from somewhere in it.

As I moved closer, I could see the car's engine literally on this young adult's lap, burning the lower extremities. The impact had been so hard that the engine broke clear off the front chassis and was pushed directly onto the kid's lap through the front dashboard of this late model, all fiberglass, built-for-speed car. It looked like the car had blown apart once it hit this tree; what we were going to be working on was the shell of the passenger compartment. Even the wheels had blown off the car.

It must have taken twenty seconds for me to regain my brain before someone else came up to me, screaming, "Come over here. He is still alive!" The same female officer grabbed my arm and led me from the car some thirty feet away into the bushes, where, unfortunately, there was another passenger with no legs who was barely breathing.

"Owen!" I looked back and saw that Owen was right where he was supposed to be, standing with a stretcher, a long board, and other spinal immobilization accessories for that poor soul.

"Take care of his airway; we'll worry about the broken bones later!"

Owen seemed to be in shock himself; we all were. Nobody even got out of their cars to help. Some slowed, rubbernecked. Finally, one motorist did stop and got out of his car—a doctor. That's when I heard the first firetruck pull up.

I left Owen with the doctor, who now was assisting us in this nightmare, then ran over to the car that was still smoldering and the screaming kid. The firefighter used the jaws of life and tried to get the engine off the patient, but it didn't seem to work due to the patient's proximity to the motor and tree.

To this day, I remember thinking this doesn't look so good.

"Do something!" Another firefighter yelled at me.

At first, I was stunned. I thought to myself, maybe I should do something, and then it hit me. What the hell am I going to do?

"Get the fucking engine off of him first!" I yelled back.

Inching closer to the wreck without getting myself killed from hot metal debris shooting from the Jaws of Life as it cut into the car, I looked down into the passenger's seat—what was left of it anyway. In it was the charred remains of another passenger.

"Jesus Christ!!" I jumped back in shock. *How many people were in this car? Maybe there are more patients.*

I frantically looked around in the trees. Yes, the trees. If one isn't wearing a seatbelt, they tend to land in strange places after being ejected from a motor vehicle crashing at high speed. At about this time, I got on the radio to let our dispatcher know our current situation, request more resources (ambulances), and to be careful gaining access to our location and not run us over because we were off the shoulder of the highway near a wooded area.

"Central, I got two critical patients, one with no legs, a DOA in the front seat, and unknown if there are any more fatalities. Also, please have a medevac standby. I'll get back to you; also, send me more units. I got to go."

Like a true professional, Mark the dispatcher did what he was supposed to do—he left me alone because he knew I was busy with whatever situation I was in. He would send help. Lots of it. In the next three to four minutes, I would have every available unit in Queens in my location helping out.

As I finished my preliminary report to Mark, a young man in his twenties tapped me on my shoulder.

"Yes, can I help you?" I raised my voice. *Is he just a random motorist?* While bad accidents happened, motorists sometimes would just leave their vehicles and walk by to see the scene. With all the screaming and the horror around, the last thing I needed was a random citizen walking around just to check things out. This guy, whoever he was, looked out of place. And he wasn't one of us; he wasn't wearing a uniform.

"What happened?" He asked in a controlled manner.

Maybe he is asking for directions? I looked behind him to see if he was indeed a motorist that had parked his car on the shoulder just to watch us work. I saw no car. Then where did he come from? In a split second, the thought dawned. "Were you in that car?" I pointed to the mangled wreck.

"Yes."

This is surreal. I blinked. "How many people were in the car?" I asked.

"I think there were four of us. Is everybody okay?"

About this time, I heard more sirens about half a

mile back on the parkway, but the units seemed to be having problems getting to this location due to the stopped traffic.

"Hey pal, if you were in that car, you're technically supposed to be dead, so do me a favor and just sit down over there." I pointed to a grassy out of the way area. "Someone will get to you in a few minutes." I started to head back over to the driver's side of the mangled car, but then I did an about-face and looked at the guy a little more closely. "By the way, are you okay? Anything hurt?" I checked to see if he had all his limbs intact.

The guy looked at me and started to wobble a little. Probably the shock of seeing the whole scene was a bit too much for him. He looked like he was going to faint, but that was a good outcome considering the condition of his other three friends.

"Just sit down, alright? You're going to be okay; I've got to go!" I headed back over to the car.

"God damn this fucking tree!" One of the fire-fighters screamed.

There was very little progress being made, and that frustrated all of us. The horrendous scream-ing from the patient only made things worse. Everyone surrounded the car.

"Look, it's hot, and it's very heavy, guys. It's a freak-ing mangled, torn-apart 425 engine! Just keep trying!" Another firefighter screamed.

What felt like an eternity was somehow measured in two to three minutes because, at that time, I turned around and saw two ambulances pulling up on the grass. Jim and Doctor Edna, who worked for Four-Two David that also covered this area, came out of the first unit. The second unit was made up of two of our senior medics, Phil and Mike. Following them in a Ford Bronco was our supervisor, Lieutenant Mattina. The vehicle looked like it had just finished taking a mud bath. Meanwhile, the rain resumed.

After taking one last look at the car, I ran over to the lieutenant's vehicle.

"Steve, my boy, what have you got?" the lieutenant asked as soon as I approached.

I described the incident to him in about thirty seconds.

"Calm down, relax, take a deep breath, take a breather, have a drink."

I wish he had a bottle.

He took over the operation and walked towards the car, where the patient was still pinned and screaming, but not as loudly as before. Progress had been made, thankfully.

"Where's Edna?" I heard the lieutenant ask Jim.

"I'm over here, Lieutenant." Edna waved. She was putting on surgical gloves.

"What are you doing over there? You're likely to get knocked down by that commotion. Come over here." He motioned for her to retreat back to his side.

"So, Stevie, how are we doing?" He asked me as I hurried over with the stretcher.

"Oh, I'm fine. You?" I responded sarcastically like we were having a little chitchat. "What do you want us to do next?"

"Well." He lit up a cigarette. "There is nothing for us to do until they get the engine off the patient, don't you agree?"

He was right—what were we to do? Jim was talking to the guy sitting on the grass, the other two medics and my partner were with the double amputee, and, well, there wasn't much we could do.

"Did you call aviation?" I reminded the lieutenant. "I think they're standing by."

The boss walked toward my ambulance, then turned to face the closed highway. He stood in the middle of the marked pavement and dialed Dispatch. He then asked me to find out the vital signs of the patient in my ambulance.

"Blood pressure fifty over ten maybe, pulse sixty,

and respirations are being assisted," I wheezed out.

Lieutenant Mattina was still talking on the radio while at the same time listening to me. "Cancel aviation. I'll get back to you." He shifted his eyes to the car, where the firefighters had begun rushing. FDNY finally lifted the engine up high enough to slide in and pull the patient out. Lieutenant Mattina took control of the operation. At the moment, he was the only person who had a grip on things. He yelled for me to get another stretcher from Jim's ambulance. He then told Phil and Mike to go to my ambulance, which had the patient with no legs. The doctor who had stopped to help Owen and us left at this point.

"BP is too low for an air ride." The lieutenant motioned to me to follow him back to the car wrapped around the tree.

"He's out!" Somebody yelled, interrupting our exchange.

"Grab the stretcher!" Lieutenant Mattina told me.

As we maneuvered towards the driver's side in between the firefighters, we held down the long board, and lo and behold, here came the stuck patient. With a little more maneuvering, he was on the stretcher. Jim and Edna hurriedly carried him towards their ambulance. "He's still alive!"

"Look, after we get the patient in Jimmy's ambulance, you take off to North Shore Hospital in your ambulance with Owen and the other two medics! I'll stay with Jimmy and Edna! I'll call in a standby for a trauma team to be waiting for you. Just go, what are you standing here for!" Mattina barked.

"Got it!" I ran to my ambulance.

"Rocky, where are his legs?" Phil asked as he opened the door.

"How the fuck should I know?"

"Take a quick look near the car. Maybe they're around somewhere. Actually, you know what, fuck the legs!" Phil followed up. "Have the other crew look around for them. We got to go; this guy is going to be dead in five minutes if we don't get him to North Shore!"

For the past five minutes, I felt like I'd been the messenger in this operation, either getting something or waiting for something. So now, getting the opportunity to leave was welcome. Just before I closed the back doors to the ambulance, I heard Pete mention that the patient just coded as a cardiac arrest.

"Shit!" I closed the doors and ran to the front of the ambulance.

I had a police escort, and I was trying to keep up with him. It was just after about two minutes I heard someone yelling from the back of the ambulance

"Holy shit, Rocky! Slow the fuck down, don't fucking kill us, for Christ's sake!"

I think at that time, my speedometer dropped down to about sixty miles per hour. I figured in two minutes or so, we should be pulling into the ambulance bay.

The trauma team was standing by and helped us get the patient out of the back of the ambulance when we arrived. They were surprised at what we brought. First of all, the patient was alive. Second, the back of the ambulance looked like we slaughtered a pig. The rear cabin, where the stretcher was, was covered in it.

"Where are the legs?" the doctor asked us while wheeling the patient into the trauma room.

"They're still looking for them," I responded.

A trauma team consists of at least six medical doctors, an x-ray technician, and two to three nurses, along with other MDs who happen to be in the triage area at the time. So, about twelve people are working to save a patient. Each has one job to do, and then there's the attending trauma physician, who is basically coordinating all of them. He's GOD. He decides when your time is up on this planet.

After about ten minutes, the doctors paused to

look at the x-rays pushed up towards the bright surgical light.

"Christ, this patient isn't even good enough for body parts," one of the physicians said.

"What's his vital signs?" the attending trauma physician asked.

"Sixty over ten, pulse fifty, ventilations being assisted," the nurse called out.

"That's surprising considering he ruptured every major organ in his body; technically, he's supposed to be dead," he said with the same tone.

"Ah...Doctor. Make the vitals forty over ten, pulse forty-eight," the same nurse called out. "Look at his pelvic area. It's filling up with his own blood." We could all see the pelvic area swell up like someone was filling up a water balloon inside his body.

The patient was bleeding internally, and there was nothing anybody could do about it.

"Looks like he's missing part of his skull also." The doctor probed the back of the head of the patient. "No lower extremities either? Contact the family. We're calling it off. Put him on a respirator. This patient was dead once he hit whatever he hit." He looked at me.

"A tree," I said.

"That'll do it. How fast?" The doctor inquired.

"I think the police said the car was doing about ninety miles per hour." I wasn't surprised at the doctor's "don't even break a sweat" attitude.

"Even his corneas are gone, kaput, mush. Too bad. We could have used them on a twelve-year-old upstairs."

As the doctors started to leave, the patient went into cardiac arrest. The team scrambled to assist him with no positive results. His heart stopped.

"Give me a time," The doctor asked the hospital administrator as the steady beeping of the machines filled the room.

"10:17 p.m.," she said.

That was the time of death that went on the certificate. About twenty minutes later, Lieutenant Mattina walked into the hospital E.R. with a red plastic bag in his hands.

"Found them! They were inside the car; can you believe it? Guy detached from them in the back seat," he said.

"I don't think he needs them now," I replied.

He sighed. "Don't tell me he's dead."

"The doc said he was braindead on impact."

"I can believe that. So, what am I supposed to do with his legs?"

"I don't know, I guess just bring them to the patient's bed." I pointed to the trauma room.

I went back to doing my paperwork as my boss walked inside the room, asking the nearby personnel where the stretcher with our patient was.

"What happened to the rest of the occupants?" I asked upon his return.

"Counting yours, that makes two dead and one in Jamaica Hospital. Their trauma team is working on the guy who was struck by the engine on his chest, and we have one walking wounded," he said to me. "The police were going to charge the driver with two deaths if he lived," he mentioned.

"What about the guy walking around?"

"He's praying by the tree, at the crash site. I left him with NYPD."

"Get out. He's still there?" I asked, very surprised. Yes, there was a little shocked chuckle too.

"Yeah, we left him. I told another unit to wait fifteen minutes, then they'll take him over to Booth Memorial hospital to be checked out, but really, he's fine. I think he was in the back seat too. The car was a convertible; he apparently flew out like a rocket and landed fifty yards away in the grass.

He said he'd had a few drinks before, and he was passed out, and when he woke up, he thought his friends were fixing a flat or something. He said he just sat there until he saw the ambulances pull up."

"Did you tell him how freaking lucky he was?" I asked the boss.

"Nope...he'll find out once the cops start asking him for a statement. Give me your logbook so I can sign it. Then why don't you guys go back to the station and decontaminate that vehicle? I peeked inside. It's very messy," he said.

"You got it, boss, and thanks for your assistance in this nightmare."

"No problem, all in a day's work, Stevie, my boy." He smiled and walked out through the sliding emergency room doors.

The drive back to the battalion was as uneventful as it could get after an intense job like we just had. Although Owen and I did get into a "little argument." We were frazzled at this point.

"Slow down! What do you want to do? Wind up like our last patient?" I was overreacting, of course. Owen was just doing the speed limit on the highway, but now we both thought we were going much too fast even though we really weren't. He decided to take the side streets back to the battalion, just in case. After decontaminating the ambulance for an hour, it was pretty much time to log off from our shift.

About fifteen minutes later, while we were in the locker room changing, one of our coworkers walked by.

"You going out tonight?" Richie Q. asked as he pushed the locker room door open.

Fashionably retro, Richie—whom I worked with at random at times when my partner was off or sick —had the neatly combed, greased-back hair look from the '50s. The thing about Rick that drove the lieutenant's crazy was also one of his talents. He would draw sketches of anything that caught his eye on a particular day. He would sometimes even draw cartoons on our prehospital care reports, which were legal documents used in court.

"Steve? Owen?" Rick asked us, tying up his moccasins.

"Oh, sure, Owen is definitely going out with us." I laughed. Owen was the kind of person that kept to himself. Hell, after working with him for over ten years, all I knew was that he had a wife and a kid. That's it. One could say it was bad on my part, not knowing my partner better. Though deep inside, I appreciated that aspect of him. I respected his privacy.

"I'll go. My wife is probably asleep anyway," I followed up while Owen, as usual, ignored us.

Darlene, my wife at the time, worked the 7 a.m. to 3 p.m. tour for the NYPD. My shift, on the other hand, was 3 p.m. to 11 p.m. So we pretty much saw each other in passing or on days off, which never worked out to our advantage because we each had different days off when working for NYC in the "public relations" or "customer service" sectors, as we would say.

"Were going to BC-2's, right?" I asked Rick, then continued to peek at Owen. "Owen's not going because he's a freaking vegetarian, but I'll meet you up there."

Owen gave me a look, grabbed his bag and jacket, then gave us the finger as he left the locker room.

BC-2's, the bar where I would sometimes meet my friends after work, was about five minutes away by car. Before I got into the driver's seat, I decided to check my trunk, where I might have had one beer left from yesterday's golf game. The temperature had dropped in the last hour to a chilly forty degrees.

I only liked cold weather because I didn't have to get ice for beers, just stuck them in my trunk—except the bottled beers. They tended to break when the weather got below freezing. Anyway, a cold one would do the trick right now.

No beer. My initial search was fruitless.

However, once I got inside the lower portion of my golf bag, I retrieved not only one but two beers in a plastic bag, still surrounded by a few ice chips. Bingo!

I popped open my beer and walked over to the driver's side, opened the door, and stared at the full moon as I took a long swig of the frosty beverage. A sudden numbness swept up the back of my throat. I hiccupped. That's not good. I either drank it too fast or was still wired up from the shift I just finished. Tonight, it was definitely a combination of both.

Upon entering BC-2's, a stranger would probably think twice before ordering a beverage. I didn't really consider it to be a dive or anything. Then again, all the patrons, including the bartender, were acting like they'd just been released from prison.

Everybody was so damn happy.

I'm talking about a good forty or so people, all New York City employees, mostly first responders of some capacity. The only thing the rundown place had going for it was that it was dark inside. After a few beers, we would feel as if we were in some ritzy establishment, which was a far cry from what this place really looked like with the lights on.

Most bars in the area catered to the divorce types, a little more upper class than the likes of us. They had a dress code—a collared shirt at the very least—and they served cocktails and such drinks. Don't get me wrong, some of us had been to places like that. We just didn't fit in there, even if we were divorced or soon-to-be, like myself.

"Rocky!" someone yelled as I opened the door and stepped inside. As I gazed across the bar looking in the direction of that last statement, a gunshot rang out. I ran for cover. I'd heard that noise a few times at work, which usually meant it was best to run in the opposite direction!

BANG! BANG! BANG! The sound of a .38-caliber revolver filled the bar.

I hurriedly crouched behind a wooded panel that separated the bar and a few tables while I regained my composure, checking my shorts for any signs of lost bowel movements.

"Target practice!" my friend screamed.

As the officer reloaded his firearm, I saw three people standing behind him. The entertainment of the moment seemed to be shooting at a moose's head that was nailed up on the wall some thirty feet away. The officer's entourage was encouraging him.

"A little to the left, you only nicked his antler this

time!" Michael, a medic from down south who worked out of the Astoria battalion, exclaimed.

"Yea, a little to the left," Suzy pointed out to the cop holding the weapon.

"Give me the gun. I'll show you how it's done." Another person motioned to the current shooter. Everybody here was no older than thirty, and we were acting like trailer park trash, myself included.

I inched closer to the mayhem and loudly proclaimed, "First of all, you guys are all fucked up. Give me the gun. I'm straight as an arrow. I'll show you how to shoot!"

They waved me off and continued drinking. I could clearly hear them planning how to accurately shoot the Moose-head beer-mascot off the wall and in between its eyes.

"I don't mean to put a damper on all this fun," I approached Mike. "But what happens when the bullet goes through the wall and blows somebody's head off?"

"Don't sweat it. There's a firewall in between this bar and the place on the other side," he said in his southern drawl. "They've been at this for about half an hour now." Mike chuckled and looked at his watch. "Besides, the store on the other side of that wall is closed. It's midnight, remember."

The next thing I know, a .38 caliber revolver is put

in my hand. "Let's see what you got!"

"You know something, I changed my mind. I think I'd rather have a beer than shoot a dead moose on the wall," I said to him.

"As you wish." The cop holstered his weapon, "I'm out of here anyway." He *gracefully* departed the establishment.

For the next two hours, we kept drinking our sorrows away, dreaming of what we would all do when we retired some fifteen years later. It was decided that "someday" we all would open up a bar, just like this place. That way, we wouldn't ever have to work again. We could just get up in the morning and go down to OUR BAR—that was the agreed-upon name of the bar.

Those days. Those times. I—I say I, but it was really all of us in the civil servant's positions—would consume alcohol until our livers exploded from all the abuse. So young, so fearless.

Sigh.

It's a shame how reality creeps up.

As usual, my first drink was a beer. With the cold bottle in my hand, I just stood in front of the counter, drinking. One of my coworkers, I can't remember his name now, approached me. "Hey, did you hear about Al"

"What happened?"

"Their ambulance was T-boned and rolled over while transporting a gunshot wound victim to the hospital."

"Yea, I heard. Some of it was on the radio. How bad was it?"

"He's in surgery now. Pretty bad. Get a load of this," he continued, "they had Navy Seal observers inside too." He chuckled. "One of the seals ended up driving the ambulance, and the other lost one of his fingers."

I sighed. "What a shit show."

About a half-hour later, Darlene, my future ex-wife, walked in. After unloading my day on her, she finally interrupted with, "I almost shot someone tonight during a vertical patrol."

"Get out of here."

"Oh, and I was by myself." She took a sip from her drink. "Hell of a day."

***

Those days were nonstop action, whether it was a car accident, a shooting, someone trying to jump out of a building to end their life, or someone slipping and falling. I behaved accordingly. I worked unending double shifts, stretching myself as thin as I could.

At times when I looked at the reflection of myself in the mirror before going to bed, I would think, "Boy, it may be time to get a haircut," or "get some Visine in those eyes. You look like a vampire."

Other times, I contemplated something along the lines of, "I think your about to go off the deep end." I would stare at my reflection, peering inside of my own mind. "You're not as smart as you think you are. I can show you, see—here's the cerebellum. After working sixteen hours yesterday and then stopping at the bar for a few drinks, you lost a shit load of brain cells. See, it's right here in the mirror."

Then I'd pass out as soon as my head would hit my pillow.

CHAPTER FIVE

Humpty Dumpty! 1994

"Four-Two-Charlie for an injury, possible Humpty Dumpty." Mark, the dispatcher's voice came from the radio speaker.

It's nice to know that some dispatchers rely on jokes to normalize a situation a tiny bit. Sometimes I would get so stressed out, wondering what kind of job I was responding to. Now at least I had an idea that our future patient fell off something, and that's why an ambulance was needed. Nine times out of ten, it was bumps and bruises or a broken arm or leg. Other times it could get pretty gruesome, like this assignment. It turned out that the patient had somehow lacerated his femoral artery mid-shaft on his left leg after falling off a ladder while trying to do some DIY remodeling.

Performing tasks of this nature is especially dangerous when no one else keeps an eye and frankly makes sure that whoever is working doesn't fall to their death. He had no one. Just a cell phone. And thank GOD for that.

My partner and I walked past the open garage of a well-kept brownstone and saw blood everywhere. It looked like someone had tipped over a gallon of red paint in the garage. Sure enough, there was this guy in his forties in a sitting position on the garage floor holding a soaked and dripping towel above his knee. I looked at my partner. He said the guy's color looked like shit, and he'd probably already lost a few pints of blood.

It was evident to me that the patient had cut his femoral artery. Bright red blood squirted out after I lifted the towel slightly off his wound to assess how bad the injury was.

"I don't feel so good." The man's voice began to fade.

"Lie down. You'll feel better." I helped him lie down, then turned to my partner.

"Throw me a bunch of four by four gauze pads and few multi-trauma dressings out of the trauma bag along with a roll of three-inch surgical tape!" Ricky made sure that was in my hands in a matter of seconds.

With the patient lying down, I lifted his left leg onto my lap, completely removed the towel, and stuck a handful of these four-by-four gauze pads into the laceration, hoping to slow the bleeding.

The gauzes did slow the bleeding but didn't stop it. I took two of the multi-trauma dressings Ricky threw my way and pressed them together on top of the gauze pads.

"Tape these in place for me," I said to Ricky while pressing them with my hand.

The new dressing was getting a little red. The patient was still bleeding. Because the tourniquets we had in the nineties were small, meant for arm injuries only, Ricky took off his FDNY/EMS-issued belt.

I wrapped it above the laceration towards the upper part of the leg, tightened it, then grabbed another dressing and taped it on top of the last blood-soaked dressings.

I looked at Ricky. "Well, that seems to be working." The patient was pretty much clueless since he was lying on his back and on the verge of passing out.

"You're going to be fine," I told him. "You might have nicked an artery, but you'll survive. DON'T PASS OUT ON ME!" I raised my voice a little more on the last part of the sentence.

He said he wouldn't, and with that, I told Ricky to go to the bus and grab the stretcher. While Ricky was getting the stretcher out of the ambulance, I asked the patient what his name was.

"Michael," he responded.

"What the fuck happened?" I asked as I put an oxygen mask on Michael. At the same time glanced at the dressings on his leg just to make sure he wasn't bleeding again.

Michael said he tried to move the ladder sideways while standing on it six feet up. Instead of coming down and moving the ladder.

"Well, we are not going to do that again, right?"

He agreed by nodding his head.

By this time, Ricky had come back. We put Michael on the stretcher and took some vital signs: blood pressure, pulse, etc. The vital signs were a little low but not as bad as I thought they would be.

He is going to make it.

As for Ricky and me, we pretty much set a speed record for stopping an arterial bleed. Another five minutes, and Michael would have bled out and died. I wrote it above, and I'll likely repeat it, no job is routine, no matter how ordinary it sounds.

WHERE THERE IS SMOKE...

In 1996 in South Jamaica, Queens, shootings were as common an occurrence as people changing socks. At least one or two 911 calls our unit responded to every day were about someone shooting someone else or themselves, accidentally or intentionally. The outcome was usually the same. Most scenes would be surrounded by total pandemonium. The bystanders screamed at us while the patient's family, the police, the FBI, politicians—everybody waited for us to perform a miracle of resurrection on a city sidewalk or in the home we were called to.

A gunshot wound to the head will plaster one's brains all over the sidewalk. Especially a high-caliber weapon. There isn't much we can do, although sometimes we had to do a little "PR work" on the patient, or else we would've been killed by an angry mob.

It was all part of a sudden rush of gunshot injuries and deaths that had gripped New York. Some of them were intentional, some were accidental. I can't speak for all the other EMTs and units, but certainly, we would get something related to a gun every week.

I first noticed that something was up while in someone's attic attending to a call for a possible gunshot wound DOA. In addition to the regular police that showed up, other agencies were there too. Their shields looked different from the usual NYPD ones I was accustomed to seeing when we were called, especially crime scenes.

After seeing these new officers a few times, I asked one of my PD friends what was up with the strange-looking shields. "They're ATF," he answered. "I think someone lost a gun shipment, and it somehow made its way here."

"What?"

"A shipment of guns heading to a gun store got lost. No one knows how, no one knows why," he explained. "But these people are losing their minds right now." He pointed to the ATF agents.

The more time passed, the more these incidents happened. Instead of the baseline of two or three gun-related crimes per day, they began to creep up to five or six. Gunpoint robberies, suicides, homicides, you name it: everything gun-related spiked.

And it showed on our calls for service as well. For about three weeks, the number of gun-related victims we treated and transported to the area hospitals increased almost daily. Sadly to say, some made it; others didn't.

It all culminated at Baisley Park—or at least I think it did, mainly because the shootings somewhat slowed down after that incident. Upon our arrival, we were notified that there were two bodies on the scene. I later found out that one was shot by a cop, and the other shot himself. While in the park, the first male had drawn and pointed a gun at an undercover ATF agent. NYPD was his backup and had intervened.

The second body was found in the lake, about fifty yards away. Single gunshot wound to the head. Though the cause of death might've been ruled something else, it looked self-inflicted. A milk crate full of guns was next to him.

CHAPTER SIX

Ourselves

Sometimes the everyday stress we all were exposed to would come out back in the station. For quite some time, two of our teams were constantly at odds with each other.

Some crews ran twenty-four hours a day. That meant three different units of two people working eight-hour shifts in the same ambulance. They were part of what we called "political busses." That generally meant that an elected official lived in the neighborhood. Sometimes the crews got on each other's nerves for not gassing up the vehicle or a million different reasons.

"Stop picking your nose and wiping it on the steering wheel. This is the last time I'm cleaning up after these Tour Two pigs. It looks like a fucking deli exploded in the front; what is the matter with these people?" Sandra Sue, who worked with EMT Unit Six-Four-Mary Tour-Three, exclaimed. Tour Two crew members had a habit of leaving the ambulance in total shambles when they finished their tour.

"Look. French fries!" She pointed to the one French fry on the floor mat in front of her passenger side.

"Are you sure they're not German fries?" Chris, her partner for over two years, squinted.

Chris, married to a cop, had spent more time with this woman than his own wife for the past year. Some of us at the station just couldn't figure out why Chris hadn't strangled Sandra yet, but she did have one significant thing going for her. Sandra was the hottest, prettiest female that EMS had. Especially in a tight uniform, I suspect she purposely ordered one size too small from the quartermaster.

Too bad for the guys that she liked women; she was a lesbian. Not that there's anything wrong with being a lesbian. There's an old saying we straight guys have: "She can't be bad if she likes women as much as we do, right?" Her girlfriends were knockouts too! She had better-looking girlfriends that most of us guys would ever see in our dreams. Guys would go crazy if she kissed whoever the girl was on any given day to pick up and drive Sandra home.

"Look, this isn't funny. Every fucking day, I'm here. I have to spend eight hours in this fucking ambulance, so is it too much to ask for them to keep it a little clean? Jesus Christ!" She raised her voice at Chris.

At about this time, Sandra went to sit down in her seat on the passenger side. Unfortunately, she forgot to pick up one other thing...an unopened ketchup packet, which exploded when she sat on it.

"Oh fuck!" She felt around her butt, then pulled out the open packet.

"That's it!" she screamed at Chris. "I'm going inside. Put us out of service!"

"What for?" Chris asked as he climbed the driver's side.

"Uniforms!" she exclaimed. "I swear I can't take it anymore!" She stomped towards the front entrance of the station.

Chris watched as Sandra left the passenger side door open and headed towards the station on a mission. "64 Mary, put us out 10-62 fuel!"

"10-4 Mary," the dispatcher confirmed.

A few minutes later, Chris and I walked into the boss's office to get the keys for the gas pumps. We suddenly realized that we had inadvertently walked into a war zone.

"I cant take it anymore! Write them up! This is the fucking tenth time, at least, where the bus is a pigsty! What is the matter with them? Are they this way at home? And look at my pants!" Sandra turned around to show the supervisor her ketchup-stained backside. She threw the remnants of the empty ketchup packet on the boss's desk.

"First of all, calm down, young lady, and close the door." He picked up the packet and noticed the red stain on her pants. "Is it that time of the month?"

Like someone had pulled the pin of a live grenade, we scurried away. I think the whole station shook when Sandra slammed the door as she left the office. And considering that it was held up by concrete cinderblocks, it likely did wobble.

CHAPTER SEVEN

The rooftop

> *"Every once in a while, you can stare into a cat's eye and make them blink."*
>
> UNKNOWN

It wasn't wise to be on the roof of an NYC housing project building; it didn't really matter which borough. At times the hallways and corridors were littered with bullet casings and syringes. Things could get a little dicey on the roof, especially if you didn't have an FDNY or NYPD uniform on.

The dispatcher gave an assignment to our unit one evening in July. "68-Adam for an unknown condition."

"Send it over," I said into the ambulance mic.

"Let me guess, someone fell, and a bystander called 911," my partner said, acting like a psychic before looking at the KDT screen.

"Does it matter?" I asked, unimpressed. By this time in my career, I had gotten enough calls that sounded mundane but turned out to be close calls.

I glanced at the address and then put the vehicle in drive. I remembered reading that it was a housing project with multiple floors, with no apartment number given and the word ROOF, typed in by a call-receiving operator.

Back in those days, most of us used the lights and sirens at our own discretion, especially when it came to so-called "low-priority" unknown conditions. In other words, I didn't have to drive like a professional race car driver.

I sometimes got a sixth sense of what I would be getting into—a vibe of some sort, a gut feeling. I didn't get a vibe on this particular call, so taking the elevator to the eleventh floor and walking up a flight of stairs to the roof at 10 p.m. seemed pretty much routine.

"I hate those fucking elevators; they always smell like piss," Darien snarled as we walked up the stairs from the eleventh floor to the roof. "I'm stepping in piss, and the elevators rattle so much I feel like the cable is gonna snap at any moment."

My partner was right. "I know; sometimes I forget to take my shoes off when I go home." Sometimes I would forget to take my shoes off when I got home, especially after stressful days, and I always regretted it.

I was the first to open the door that led to the roof, my partner trailing me. At first glance, nothing seemed to be amiss or out of place. Just a plain roof—with a beautiful view of NYC, I might add.

Every so often, one's brain would suppress disturbing images when they fleetingly flash by. This time, nothing was suppressed in my mind. I saw a young girl, maybe fourteen or fifteen years old, standing on the ledge, crying, on the far side of the roof.

"Fuck it…it's a 90. Let's get out of here." My partner Darien took a step back toward the other side of the door. He didn't see what I saw.

Shocked and unable to act, I initially just stared at the distressing view. I was pretty much frozen in my tracks. As I snapped out of it, I nudged Darien and pointed to the girl. I didn't want to scare her.

"Shit!" Darien muttered.

We both had forgotten about our radios; they were at maximum volume. And, of course, Murphy's law kicked in. The dispatcher's voice blared through both our portables, asking for an update. We panicked and reached for our radios, lowering the volume.

At this point, I thought the girl had to hear that someone else was up on the roof with her. And she probably did hear the radio transmission but disregarded it—possibly because she was contemplating taking her own life.

I looked at Darien, who looked as if he was frozen to the sticky roof tar. Instinctively I stepped forward and stopped some fifty feet away.

"Hello, miss?" I raised my voice enough for her to hear me.

The young woman didn't acknowledge me; she just continued crying.

I didn't want to make any sudden moves, or even breathe. I was afraid to startle the young lady and make her jump.

Unsure what to do next, I just blurted, "Lady, you can't be standing on the ledge like that. Can you please come down?" That was probably the worst thing I could've said. Nobody wants someone to move when they are standing on a ledge twelve floors up, so I followed up with, "Wait, don't move!"

I looked over at Darien, who was shaking his head at my verbal techniques on how to talk down a suicidal patient.

"Can I come over and talk to you for a second?" I asked the young lady.

Believing she nodded, "okay," I slowly walked toward her and soon was standing next to the young woman. The ledge was the only barrier between us.

"Do me a favor, please," I pleaded with the young lady. "Can you grab my hand?" I put my hand out.

She definitely nodded "okay" this time. I moved my hand closer to hers. She took it.

As soon as I felt her hand in mine, I clutched it. She's not going anywhere. *I'm not letting go until she comes off the ledge.* I grabbed her forearm with my other hand. "This is a pretty bad place to stand, wouldn't you say?" I said as I slowly pulled the young lady down next to me.

As Darien helped her get onto the other side of the ledge, I turned around and looked up at the sky. "Thank you, God!" I nervously lit up a cigarette.

I gave Darien a few minutes to talk to the girl, then walked over. She said her name was Elaine and she lived in this building on the sixth floor.

"Give Central an update. We're taking the stairs, not the elevator." Darien helped the young lady up, escorting her to the roof door.

I grabbed all of our equipment and followed them.

Six floors down, we ended up meeting Elaine's grandmother. We explained the situation and told her Elaine needed to speak to someone at the hospital. She fully agreed to, then mentioned that Elaine had been "acting out" and that she had seen a doctor before.

I asked her if Elaine had requested medical help for any type of depression, which was evident to me at this point.

"No, never," she responded. Her grandmother then mentioned something about acne and thought that Elaine didn't feel pretty anymore. That was why she was "acting out."

"Acne?" I asked, pretty much flabbergasted.

Is this what this is all about? Acne!

At times we zip through life at breakneck speed. Work, bills, schedules, all of that can have a grave toll on those around us. Sometimes I wish I was never in this profession but knowing that I just saved a life made it worthwhile.

CHAPTER EIGHT

Cats and baby powder.

I wasn't above rushing through life. I personally never got a chance to stop and smell the roses. I was either going to be late for work, or I just want to leave as fast as possible when my shift is over.

However, whenever I did happen to be early to work, I would check out the surrounding blocks around the station. After several years of driving in and out of work, I'd noticed a dozen or so people regularly walked down Parsons Boulevard. It seemed as if it was routine for this group. Rain or shine, winter or summer, these same people walked around together.

"Hi. I'm just curious. I see you guys and girls all the time walking. What's it all about?" I finally pulled over and asked a young woman, one of the group members, who at the time walked closer to me.

"It's a marathon," the young woman in her twenties answered.

"How long is it?" My curiosity itched.

"25,000 miles. That's the circumference of the Earth. We walk for peace," she told me, then left me and rejoined the group.

Her group was part of Sri Chinmoy's, sort of a Hare Krishna-type. The original leader of this peaceful movement was from India. He moved to NYC sometime in the sixties. As far as I could tell, they were prominent vegetarians and very business-oriented. Nice people. Since they couldn't actually run around the globe, they ran, or powerwalked, around the same square block five thousand times.

As I pulled away, confused at what I just heard from the young lady, I muttered, "25,000 miles? Running in circles, are they freaking nuts?"

Just before I pulled into the station parking lot, I saw the headlines for the day from our friendly neighborhood religious fella.

"BROTHER KILLS BROTHER OVER GOD'S LAND, DUST IS OUR HOME: Abraham's sons Isaac and Ishmael." Day in–day out, he stood on the corner, holding a sign.

Spreading the word of god, I presume.

I shook out of my inner thoughts and looked at my watch. "Shit, I'm going to be late. Here we go again."

I walked into the station at precisely 4 p.m. and began my usual everyday interactions with my co-workers, accentuated by Sandra. She was particularly salty today. After losing a shouting match with the supervisor, she stormed past me.

I changed and got the keys for the ambulance I was going to operate for the day, then walked outside. A cat ran in front of me and hid past the fence. It wasn't a secret that the furry animals had claimed the hospital grounds as their realm. At times, I thought I was the one trespassing on their territory.

Sunning themselves on our vehicle's hoods, shading themselves under the ambulances... everywhere I looked, there would be one sitting or walking. They weren't even those nice cats who purr and come up to you to rub on your leg like they do in those animal commercials. No, these cats, these were cats from hell. The week before, I'd seen one with half of its freaking scalp missing, walking around like some kind of macabre death-cat from Pet Sematary.

Having two cat ladies that fed them didn't help either. One of them strolled by in the morning; the other, around five p.m. Like the pied piper, as soon as they show up, all the cats came out.

Now don't get me wrong, I'm not an animal hater or anything like that; I like cats. But at times, too much was, well, too much. Shaking my head, I entered the recreation room.

"Is that a cat?" I pointed to a hairy creature on the couch.

"Yep, that's the lampshade cat," Owen said. "You know, when them cats get an infection in their ear or something, they put that lampshade thing on, so they won't scratch."

The furry animal followed my every movement as I walked into the room.

"Look, everybody chipped in because they felt sorry for the damn thing. Hell, Joe from 21-Frank took the cat to the vet on his own time."

I looked around the perimeter at which I was standing. I glanced at the garbage and saw a sheet of tin foil someone had discarded after eating a sandwich or something. I picked it up, crumpled it into a ball, and tossed it at Owen's head. It bounced off it and landed inside the cat's lampshade cone.

"SCORE!" I shouted as the cat darted out of the door.

"That was not a very nice thing to do."

"It wasn't meant for the cat. Still. God knows what kind of things the feline has picked up; besides, it has fleas!" I pled my case.

I walked to the door and saw the lampshade feline entering the nearest point of shelter: 64-Mary ambulance. The vehicle Sandra was going to operate for the day. Witnessing the cat inside the back of the ambulance, Gary and Mike, who were clearing the car, closed the door, locking it inside the rear cabin.

"How pissed do you think she'll get?" They both laughed, trying to keep a straight face.

I'm sure they're going to let it out before the new crew gets in. Shaking my head, I headed for the boss's office to sign out a radio.

"Hey Rocky, she come in yet?" Gary asked me as I passed the office's door frame.

I knew he was asking me about Sandra. "Yeah, she's in the back changing."

"They gave me a command discipline." Mike wasn't happy. "Both Gary and I are being fined one day's pay, about $300, for keeping the ambulance in unsanitary conditions."

"Ouch." I grabbed a radio from the dock. "Hey, listen, are you going to let that cat out of the..."

"Ahhh! Shit! Get it off me! This fucking thing! Get it off!" Sandra's loud shriek penetrated the entire station.

Both Owen and I rushed outside to the parking lot to see one crew member fighting off a cat stuck on her jacket with a lampshade on its head and her partner covered in white dust or something. Whatever the dust was, it was still coming out of the front cab part of the ambulance.

"Get this fucking cat off me!" Sandra screamed at us. As Owen and I ran over, Chris brushed himself off and swearing at the top of his lungs.

Owen first took a swat at the cat with his portable radio, hitting the lampshade part attached to its neck. Just like that, the cat came off Sandra's jacket and ran away. I just stood there amazed, trying to figure out what the hell was going on.

The next thing I knew, Chris was talking to me. Well, he wasn't really talking to me. He was making his impression of a raging lunatic, and I was trying to understand what he was saying as spit was flying from his mouth.

"Take it easy... Take it easy...." I tried to calm him down.

"I'm going to kill them! I swear to God...I mean...

I'm a man of God, BUT I'm going to kill them!" Chris was covered with white stuff all over his face and the front portion of his jacket. I quickly surmised it was powder.

"Relax, it's only baby powder," I said to Chris after taking a whiff of it.

"It's what?" Chris stopped swearing.

"Baby powder," I said again, looking inside the vehicle over his shoulder.

Likely to get back at them, the Tour Two crew must have poured the baby powder down all the air conditioning vents and pointed them toward where the next crew occupants would be sitting. So, when the vehicle was turned on, and the fans spun. Poof! Powder city!

At about this time, the lieutenant walked outside to do what we called *a gasoline check*. He stopped, looked at us, and noticed Chris covered in baby powder.

"Are we all logged on, children?" He completely ignored the fact that Chris was trying to get the baby powder off his uniform.

"Yes, Lieutenant!" We answered together, pretending nothing happened in the last few minutes.

"Well then, get the hell out of here and head to your sectors." He stood for a moment looking at us, waiting to witness us getting in the ambulances and driving away. The boss then continued his quest to figure out if the station needs more fuel for the vehicles. He clearly saw that some of us were covered in baby powder, and the cats were scurrying away but didn't comment on it. And none of us complained about what happened, maybe because we all expected him to say something. I wasn't going to say anything. I wasn't involved in any of this.

"Don't say a fucking word to anyone about this!" Sandra demanded, directing her statement to Owen and me.

"About what?" I asked, jumping in the passenger side of my ambulance.

These episodes were intense when they happened, but they made our lives that much more exciting and bearable in retrospect. Here I am, almost twenty years later, contemplating a bunch of coworkers playing pranks on each other. Giggling while I think about them, I might add.

CHAPTER NINE

The difference

Being in the right place at the right time can make all the difference in the world. Every once in a while, we can put a smile on someone's face, intentional or not.

Queens' Dispatch received a call for a confirmed shooting on a freezing February night and realized one of his units, us, was around the corner from where the call originated. We had just dropped off a patient at the hospital.

"34 Charlie, are you still at Metro South Hospital?"

"Pretty much. What's up, Central?" I said into my portable radio

"It's Saturday night in the big city. Here's your last job; you actually might get off on time tonight."

"Sounds good to me. Send it over." Dispatch gave out the location over the air and sent it to our computer in the ambulance.

At this point, my partner Phillips was bullshitting and standing in the ambulance bay, trying to figure out how to close a compartment stuck in the open position. After a few kicks, the compartment was fixed; it was closed permanently, or at least until the next crew figured out how to pry it open again.

Another crew, 34 Victor, was coming out of the hospital when they heard the dispatch call.

"You want back-up?" they offered.

"The more, the merrier," I said as I jumped into the bus—that's what we called the ambulances—with Phillips at the wheel. 34 Victor told Dispatch to put them on our back as well, and off we went to a location that was basically one block away.

It was a confirmed shooting, and according to the information, it was unknown if the person who did the shooting was still on the scene and that we should wait for NYPD before gaining entry.

I looked at my partner and read the job on the screen to him while he drove, lights and sirens on, and asked, "Do you really want to wait for PD?"

Phillips looked at me. "Fuck no!"

"Exactly!" The job was literally around the corner from the hospital—I mean, it took us two minutes to go up the street and make a right, then go one block and make another right and drive down a dead-end road with two rows of houses.

After turning on our searchlight to illuminate the house addresses, we saw a middle-aged woman walking towards us. She was holding what seemed to be a towel of some sort on the face of a middle-aged gentleman.

As they saw us coming, both of them headed quickly to my side of the ambulance.

"At least they are walking," Phillips said.

I got out of the ambulance and approached them. "What happened?"

"I think he was shot!" The woman moved the towel to show me a very small laceration to the man's cheek, close to the nose region. I took out my flashlight and looked closely. There was hardly any blood; it could easily be mistaken for almost any-thing—except a bullet wound.

It took my partner asking for a second time, "What

happened?" for the man to finally answer.

"Someone shot me."

Phillips put his hand on the back of the man's head and then showed me. No blood on his hand. It meant that if it was a gunshot wound, also called a GSW, there was an entrance wound but no exit. Not a good sign. I told the guy to come inside the ambulance so I could take a closer look.

By the time the man got into the ambulance, Phillips had already taken out our trauma bags and thrown the longboard on the stretcher. I told the patient to just sit down and let me check him out. At about this time, the crew of 34 Victor came walking up and asked Phillips what was going on. Phillips pointed to me.

I was talking to the patient sitting on our stretcher while taking his blood pressure and pulse. The patient was totally coherent, and then like a light switch, his color changed from normal to gray, and he went into cardiac arrest.

I looked at my coworkers. "I think the guy was shot in the face."

"Shit...must be a .22 caliber," Phillips said.

"The last reading of the blood pressure was 90 over 60. The rate was a buck-fifty. He must have just bottomed out and gone into arrest; the patient has no freaking pulse whatsoever now," I said.

I told Phillips to notify the trauma team at Metro for a traumatic arrest GSW to the head and grabbed Tommy from 34 Victor. "Have the girl go with your partner in your bus. You come with me. We got to go now." With that, Phillips made a U-turn and headed back to Metro Hospital.

I looked at Tommy and asked, "You want to start IV line of something?"

"Are you kidding? I'll hook him up to the heart monitor, start CPR, and use the BVM (Bag Valve Mask). You hook it up to the portable oxygen, and we'll shock him at least once. In ninety seconds, we'll be back in the E.R," he replied.

We came around the corner, and I stood clear as Tommy shocked the patient. Our heart monitor actually showed the patient had a heart rate now, but not enough to stop doing CPR. A few minutes later, we rolled in the back entrance of the E.R and met the same doctor who had treated our last patient fifteen minutes ago. He looked at us as we quickly wheeled the current patient into the E.R.

"Didn't I just see you guys?" The doctor said as we stopped the stretcher in front of him.

The trauma team came rushing in and took over. They hooked the patient up to the monitors; I saw that he did have a pulse—very faint, but he was alive. So, they continued CPR and started pushing drugs through a just-established IV line, then intubated him.

I gave a verbal report from what I surmised and then left to avoid being in the way. I looked at Phillips. "I need a fucking drink."

"You and me both," he replied.

I went to a desk and started my Actual Call Report (ACR). About halfway through, the lady who had been walking out the guy who was shot came over to me, threw her arms around me, and said, "Thank you."

I recognized her and said that her friend was in good hands and that he was alive, and I sincerely wished them both good luck.

A few months later, Phillips and I got a Prehospital Save Medal for this assignment.

Apparently, we do make a difference.

***

It was the summer of the year 1995. A nice and warm day, I might add. I got off from the usual shift of ferrying injured patients to the hospital, got in my car, and drove home.

A strange echo reverberated throughout the apartment I shared with my wife, Officer Darlene, as I entered and turned the lights on. Something was out of the ordinary.

My bedroom was empty. I took a deep sigh.

She left me.

My cat jumped from the couch and roamed the open space where my bed used to be. I dropped my bag on the floor, walked to the refrigerator, and picked a beer. Opening it, I sat on the living room couch. This bitch had the balls to do this after I trusted and believed in her when nobody else did!

"Fuck it." I cried myself to sleep.

I woke up to the sound of my phone ringing. It was 6 a.m.

"Hey Rocky, you want to do a tour change? Johnson called in sick. You can work a day tour and be off for the late…and the Station checks come out today," Lieutenant Quines said as soon as I picked up the handle.

"How's the weather out?" I asked, half-asleep

"It supposed to be in the eighties," he said enticingly.

I sighed. "Give me an hour."

"10-4." The lieutenant sounded relieved.

I realized that at this point, my life sucked. I then

fell back onto the couch and pulled the covers over my head, hoping this all was a bad dream.

It wasn't.

***

Driving to work that day was brutal. Knowing that my marriage went down the crapper, I hoped for some divine intervention to hit me. After graduating from her academy, Darlene's demeanor changed. At times she would demand to do things I couldn't do or flatly didn't want to. All along, we had money issues, but I thought we were managing them reasonably well. Couple all of that with the way she would talk to me, and I began second-guessing myself. *Maybe I am the prick she said I was.*

CHAPTER TEN

The Nitropaste incident (1995)

As my shift ended, I drove the ambulance up 164th Street. I saw the religious fella again, white robe and all. His divine words of wisdom for the day: "CHAPTER 12 OF THE BOOK OF THE LORD SAYS HE LONGS FOR DEATH FOR THE SINS OF HIS CHILDREN."

I would generally read his messages as I would roll in for work, but because I did a day tour that day the order in which my general events would go was reversed. I pulled into the parking lot and got out of the car. As far as the routine went, work was the same on the day shift as during the usual after-noon tour I was accustomed to. Except the sun was out! Ah yes, also, all the coworkers I knew were now coming in to work as I was getting out.

I saw Sandra get out of her car coming in to work. I waved to her, but she didn't seem to notice me, and I seriously no longer cared.

After doing my usual sign-out routine, I walked out of the station and headed to my personal car. Suspiciously, Sandra and Chris were standing on the corner, observing the late shift crew they had become so *fond of* over the last two weeks. They were getting their equipment off the ambulance.

A few words were exchanged, which was strange considering they couldn't stand each other.

Who the hell knows, maybe they kissed and made up? It's not my problem anyway.

Getting into my car, I depressingly realized that golf was not even an option today due to my cur-rent marital status. Other than maybe drinking and staring at my empty walls, I had pretty much nothing to do at two o'clock on a beautiful Tuesday afternoon. I just sat in my car for a few moments, trying to figure out what the hell I was going to do with the rest of the day.

As Kenny and Mark walked towards me, I saw them laughing and doing the usual spoiled brat routine.

"Mark and I are going to have a few beers over at Fillmore's."

"Yeah, have fun. I don't think so, not today."

Normally I would have jumped at the chance to have a few beers. However, I decided that drinking alone would be much more tolerable.

Kenny's car wasn't parked too far from mine, and as he approached it and grabbed the handle to open the door, the strangest thing happened. He collapsed—no, I don't mean he collapsed, I mean he fucking went down like a wet sack of potatoes. One moment he was standing, and the next, he was kissing the pavement.

What the hell just happened?

I instinctively got out of my car and ran toward him, screaming, "10-85! Get a stretcher! Stat!" *Christ! Did he have a stroke or something?* "Get the hell over here! I think your partner just stroked out!" I shouted at Mark, who was a few car lengths over.

Mark and I knelt next to him and turned him over. A few coworkers came running over with a stretcher. The lieutenant followed the gathering coworkers to see what just happened.

"What's going on?" Someone asked as he rushed

and knelt next to me.

"I don't know. He was standing there. Next thing I know, he just collapsed!" I reported.

"I have a pulse. It's a little weak, but he has one!" Mark grabbed Kenny's wrist.

"Kenny, Kenny, can you hear me?" His partner screamed into his ear as Kenny began to come around.

As Kenny waved him off—I actually think he went to punch him—everybody calmed down a little bit. Jesus, in like thirty seconds, about twenty medics had rushed at Kenny's side. As he became conscious, everybody kind of dispersed, except for a few of us.

"No need to have ten units on the scene for one patient. 42 X-ray, you stay." He commanded two medics in uniform next to him. "The rest of you, if you're logged on, get out of here!" The lieutenant laid down the law. He knelt and got closer to Kenny. "Now, son, what was the last thing you remember doing?"

Kenny was still a little groggy, but he pointed to the door handle.

The lieutenant looked at the handle, then proceeded to put his hand on it. Almost as if he touched a live wire, he immediately pulled his hand away and looked at it.

"Damn!" He wiped his hand on his shirt a few times. "What is that?"

I saw the lieutenant scan the rest of us who remained on the scene. He looked at Chris and Sandra standing there in the back.

The lieutenant, or as I called him "the Smoking Joe," gestured with his index finger to both to get closer to him. *Do you mean us?* The two shrugged.

Lieutenant nodded his head with a "yes," and smiled.

As the two walked over, Joe asked Sandra to open Kenny's door and get his keys. Kenny still had his keys; he hadn't gotten inside the car.

Sandra and Chris looked at each other, then said that they didn't think it was a good idea to go inside somebody's personal vehicle without permission.

Joe yelled down to Kenny, "Kenny, my boy, Miss Sandra will be entering your car. Is that okay, son?"

"As long as she's not armed," Kenny muttered.

"Ha! Only if she's not armed, what a kidder!" I added. We all let an awkward and nervous chuckle.

The Lieutenant, however, was not laughing. "Would one of you mind opening that door, please?"

Neither Chris nor Sandra wanted to open the door.

"What's all the fuss about who wants to open the door?" Mark, Kenny's partner, stepped in and went to open the door. The lieutenant caught his arm mid-flight. He directed one last statement to the pair in question: Chris and Sandra.

"Nitropaste?" He angrily asked.

It's hard for me to explain the scene I witnessed without making an allegory. Imagine you walk into a room where your pet bird should be inside a cage. You find the cage open. The only other being inside is your cat, and it shrugs its shoulders as feathers stick out of its mouth.

That's what Sandra and Chris looked like. The guilt was painted all over their smirking faces.

The lieutenant fumed as he got to his feet. "I want all four of you in my office now!"

"What about Kenny?" I asked.

"Drag his ass in if you have to!" he told me over his shoulder.

Nitropaste is a medication used to treat medical conditions related to blood circulation issues. I surmised that either Sandra or Chris put some of that gel on Kenny's car door handle. When it met his skin, it quickly opened his body's blood vessels. So, when the Nitro took effect, it momentarily drained some blood from his brain. Usually, the body will compensate for the drain, and the person will gain consciousness in a matter of thirty seconds or so.

Do not try this at home!

Most of us who witnessed the fall had no idea of what occurred after, but what happened next in the boss's office was kind of funny. Someone had helped Kenny and three other poor souls into the clutches of a possibly deranged lieutenant who basically couldn't take this shit anymore, and he let them know it.

Twenty minutes later, the four medics, including Kenny, exited the office. It was then that we knew it was safe to return if we wanted to. As everyone went downstairs, I helped Kenny back to his car, wondering its turn to possibly get pranked the day after.

All four of them left in separate directions toward their cars, each holding a slip of paper. A Command Discipline slip. Then I saw Mark wiping down his car door handle not too far away.

"That was worth every penny," Sandra mumbled with a mischievous grin on her face. She got into her 1990 Firebird and sped off.

That Command Discipline cost Chris and Sandra $250 each.

CHAPTER ELEVEN

Changes

I n 1995, NYC EMS began a merge with the NYC Fire Department. Many people were either transferred to different stations, got promoted, retired, or were let go due to their chronic fuckups. FDNY was NOT going to tolerate recreational drug or alcohol abuse, especially when it came to running over civilians under the influence on their days off. NYPD has had this ongoing problem with drugs and alcohol. Their solution was to voluntarily check themselves in to a drug and alcohol rehabilitation and stay for treatment for thirty days. It was the same procedure as we had, as long as no one got hurt

Some people at the station remained. I was happy there, although my personal life still sucked.

Thank god for my little brother, Craig, who lived in Fresh Meadows. He let me move into his studio apartment with nothing but a few bags of clothes. Even at my age, those experiences taught me about loyalty, friends, and family, which I am fortunate and proud to have. My brother did what I would've done for him. My friends supported me any way they could.

THE ORANGE JUICE INCIDENT.

Methadone is substituted for heroin for those who wish to kick the habit. Unfortunately, all it does is replace one wrong for another. Not that I could come up with something better.

Patients flocked to Queens's General Hospital three times a week and lined up outside a trailer to get their cocktail: orange juice and methadone. No matter what the weather was, you could set your watch by them; 7:00 a.m. The addicts showed up religiously for their cocktail, and if they didn't, they were either dead or back on shooting heroin.

After they had their treatment cocktail, they were so fucked up it's not funny. You talk about a staggering drunk. These people were ten times worse; the only difference was that they never fell!

Heroin, on the other hand, makes your body so relaxed you stop breathing. That's usually when I ran into these people—shooters, usually in respiratory arrest, or just about to go into.

What we did is give them a medication, NARCAN, that basically reversed their high. I can't tell you how many times we'd been cursed at for saving a heroin addict's life.

I remember one time coming to work in a thunderstorm. I stopped at the light and there, in full view, was a methadonian with car cables in his hand standing in the pouring rain, almost passed out, while his partner was sitting behind the wheel passed out as well. Now you should know that this was a pretty busy intersection, but nobody did anything.

Forty-five minutes later, while leaving the hospital grounds with our ambulance, we saw the same two guys, and they still hadn't moved a muscle. It was simply amazing.

THANK GOD nobody was *kind* enough to give them a jump.

Now, I spoke about Methadone and its uses because sometime in the mid to late '90s, I stayed at my recently acquainted girlfriend Mary's house for a few months. Unbeknownst to me, she was a "methadonian." On Fridays, the clinic would give them double the dose. For the weekend (clinics closed on the weekends), the patient would have to take the Sunday dose independently.

The methadone they would administer was mixed with orange juice. One day I got up at six in the morning at her place. The first thing I did after I went to the bathroom was hit the refrigerator. I was thirsty from a night of abusing my liver. When I saw the big Styrofoam cup of orange juice, I naturally drank the whole thing and went back to bed.

I walked around like a zombie for four days. Needless to say, it took me years before I actually resumed drinking orange juice again.

CHAPTER TWELVE

Cambria Heights General /EMS Station 45 / 1997-98

After the merge, I worked with a new partner and a new unit, but I was still working in the same area.

"54 Eddie, please respond over to Creedmoor Hospital for an emotionally disturbed person," Mark assigned us.

"10-4," I responded.

"Isn't that a psychiatric hospital?" Mark Daniels, my partner for the day, asked.

"Yes, it is. What's your point?"

"Don't hospitals have, you know, doctors?" My partner today has just come out of the academy, and this is probably his first "real job."

"Look, I've gone through this a dozen times. For some reason, before the patients can be admitted to a psychiatric hospital, they have to be medically cleared and told by a psychiatrist at a regular hospital that they're mentally disturbed," I explained.

Mark looked at me. "This job is really fucked up."

"Welcome to the real world, pal."

As we pulled in, we saw the hospital security guard direct us to Building 40, which lay on the other side of the hospital grounds. We passed the thirty-foot-tall Christmas tree the patients helped decorated, and we stopped and looked at it for a moment.

"You know, you almost have to look at it sideways to get that Christmassy effect."

"It's not bad, considering everyone here is on heavy-duty medication," Mark politely remarked.

"Did you notice the hockey mask where the star should be?"

"Where?" He strained his neck, looking up as we passed it.

The call was for an OB/labor—basically, someone pregnant. The patient we went to pick up was in labor; her contractions were five minutes apart. The physician on the scene told us to take her to the hospital. That sounded easy enough. To tell you the truth, the patient wasn't that bad. I was playing doctor for the shift, so I was in the back while Mark drove. I even had a conversation with her. It wasn't till she told me who the father was that I started to, how should I put this? Get scared!

"So, do you want to guess who the father is?" She said after staring at me for a few minutes.

The patient, maybe twenty-five years old, was white with blonde hair. She seemed to have one slight problem; she liked burning down places where she lived.

"I don't know. Is he famous?" I asked.

"Yes, sort of." She smiled at me almost flirtatiously.

I played along. "I don't know; I give up."

"Satan!" Her eyes bulged out.

"Oh really." I nervously started to pay attention to her now.

She grabbed my ear with her left hand. "I'm telling you the truth. Lucifer is the father of my baby!"

"Oh, really, and where did you two meet?" I asked

sarcastically, slowly removing my ear from her grasp.

"I was raped by him in a deserted subway station. He saw me waiting for a train, and with his red glowing eyes, he summoned me to follow him through the dark tunnel past the subway station."

At this point, she looked at me, and I swear to god I thought her head was going to spin around.

"Don't you believe me?" she said, acting like she was a twelve-year-old child, lost and in need of sympathy.

I tried ignoring her. "Whatever you say, darling."

She started chanting something bizarre and very softly, but loud enough for me to hear it.

"Hey chauffeur, you want to drive a little faster?" I leaned forward and asked Mark. "The patients' contractions are getting closer—two minutes apart."

"10-4," I heard from up front.

"AHHHHHHHHHHHH!!!!!!!!!!!!" Her eyes were almost popping out as she screamed.

"AHHHHHHHHHHHHHH!!!!!!!!!!!!" I screamed back, staring at her. My eyes were wide open in fear as well.

"Is everything alright back there?" I heard Mark

ask with a concerned voice.

"Just drive faster!" I yelled.

In two minutes, we were at the hospital, and the patient was out of our hands and on the way to labor and delivery.

Mark walked up to me as I was washing my hands and face at a nearby sink. "Hey, you okay? You look a little pale."

"Yeah, well, you'd be a little pale if you had the Antichrist in the back of your ambulance."

"What?" Mark didn't really understand what I was talking about.

"Forget it," I said, walking away. Mumbling to myself, I exited the hospital ER to smoke a cigarette. I swear, people want to know why I drink. Well, this was the reason, number 666. That's why I drink.

CHAPTER THIRTEEN

Candles and cheap cologne.

A few sections in South Jamaica, the Queens area where I used to work, were quite lovely! Back in the '30s and '40s, many of the jazz musicians from that era lived around there.

"Four-Two Zebra for an injury coming over to your screen." That was our dispatcher calling another unit.

"10-4." I could hear Vicky, an EMT from a private hospital with its own ambulance department, in the 911 system.

"Four-Two Charlie, maybe you can back up Four-Two Zebra. They just upgraded the job," Queens Dispatch assigned us.

"10-4. Fax it over to the screen."

Because Bobby, my partner, had taken the day off that day, Laurie was my partner. She had about seven years on the job at the time, was about my height, 5'7", and had a great personality.

When we arrived on the scene about five minutes later, an FDNY firefighter was standing in the living room with a hose pointed at our patient, ready to wash her down.

The water pressure in a hose like that would punch her through the wall. I figured in about three seconds, our patient was about to be blown through the kitchen wall unless somebody opened their mouth real fast.

"Time out, guys!" Vicky from Four-Two Zebra yelled at the top of her lungs as soon as she entered the room. Vicky, who we were dispatched to supplement, was a short but beautiful woman, and she could handle herself quite well in the streets. Her partner was like her bodyguard; he reminded me of Mr. T.

We took control of the situation, taking the woman's clothes off and wrapping her with burn sheets. A burn sheet is a packaged sterile piece of cloth that is designed to prevent infections, especially with burn victims. Vicky started an IV drip, and we placed the patient on a stretcher and transported her to NYU Medical Center in Manhattan. She was admitted with eighty-five percent second-degree burns and fifteen percent third-degree burns over her whole body.

There's a moral to the story: don't wear cheap cologne and walk by candles.

After an hour in the hospital, between paperwork and bringing the patient up to the burn unit and restocking with what we could "borrow" from NYU Medical Center, we got back to the ambulance. At that point, our primary goal was to get out of Manhattan and into Queens, the borough where our unit actually belonged.

We opened the back doors of the ambulance simultaneously. "We can't go back into service; the ambulance smells like we barbequed our last patient," my partner said after she covered her nose.

I peered in and took a whiff. "Smells like my hands from last year when I went to pick up my muffler when it fell off."

"What?" Bobby asked, closing one side of the door.

"Remember, last year I told you my muffler came off on the parkway, and I pulled over and ran back a few yards to retrieve it," I said.

"Vaguely."

"I pulled over to the shoulder of the parkway and thought, I can't afford another muffler. I'll just run back and get the one that just fell off the car. Maybe some mechanic can solder it back on or something. So off I went and ran back about fifty yards or so, and I picked the muffler with my bare hands up and started running back to my car on the shoulder of the parkway. "I was wondering where someone was having a barbeque because it smelled like someone was cooking a steak," I said with a chuckle.

Bobby sighed. "You know you're not supposed to pick up a muffler with your bare hands after it falls off a running car."

I shrugged and returned to the problem at hand. "The back of the ambulance smells like burnt flesh." I'll never forget that smell; I could not escape it for a month, ugh. "Tell Queens Dispatch we're going out of service. Reason: blood-borne pathogens. The whole back of the bus needs to be decontaminated. If any boss gives us a problem, they can stick their head in the back and take a deep breath," I concluded.

"You got that right," Bobby said, closing the back door of the ambulance.

After telling the dispatcher our unit was out of service, we headed back to our station in Queens. We figured it was a good forty-five-minute drive because of the traffic. During that time, I told Bobby I never really got the chance to properly thank him for helping me move twice in the past three years after being abandoned by my wife and my last girlfriend after the orange juice incident.

"No problem, bro, that's what friends are for, and you would do the same for me." He laughed. "You know, there was an inside bet with the bosses that you were going to be taken out, shot by either your wife or your latest."

I laughed as well. "I would have taken that bet."

After arriving back to our station on that sweltering summer evening in mid-July, both Bobby and I finished decontaminating the back of the ambulance with a power hose—and a lot of bleach, I might add.

Bobby and I had soaked T-shirts on with our wet uniform pants, and we looked and smelled like somebody had pulled us out of the washing machine during the rinse cycle. At this point, we were on overtime. Nobody really wanted to stay at work after their shift was over, and it was nearing the time of tour change. So, personnel were either dropping partners off from other stations or leaving to pick up partners at other EMS stations. This happened more often than one would think; you have to remember our agency was always short-staffed, and when personnel called in sick, bosses had to swap members around. After all, we weren't real people. We were just shield numbers.

About this time, Maryellen from another EMS station pulls up in an ambulance to pick up Sandra Sue. "Hit Me Baby One More Time" by Britney Spears was coming from the ambulance's radio, filling the vicinity.

At first, I didn't recognize her, but she looked over at me when she stopped the ambulance and smiled. Sandra Sue jumped in the passenger seat when the ambulance stopped and punched in the shield numbers on the ambulance computer.

I smiled and blew Maryellen a kiss; she grabbed it in midair and gestured for me to come over to the driver's side of the ambulance. I had a crush on her when we were in the academy, and I'm pretty sure she knew it. There was a time she stuck up for me to my NYPD wife, and academically she helped me in the study group regarding procedures and EMS protocols. She was beautiful—and unfortunately, married.

I walked to her side of the ambulance and leaned on her window. She looked me in the eye, moved her index finger up to her lips, then put it into her mouth very slowly and very sensuously. After taking it out very deliberately, she pulled me by my wet T-shirt closer to her. She then took her index finger out of her mouth, slowly traced my lips, and put it back in her mouth. She closed her eyes and let a shallow, quiet moan that apparently every living creature on this planet could hear.

I swear, you could have heard a pin drop. All personnel standing outside at the time watching this encounter reminded me of what a deer looked like when caught in the headlights of an oncoming car. They were all staring. Sandra Sue, Maryellen's partner for the shift, was even leaning over to see this *R-rated* action happen, and you just knew it was going to be a girl week for her. From what I heard after, Lieutenant Louis, one of our supervisors, was standing outside watching this with his mouth open himself.

It was then one of the medics casually walked up to the lieutenant and told him that a female praying mantis usually bites the head off the male partner after they have sex.

"Is that a fact?" The boss stared. Poor Lieutenant Lewis: I bet you at the time he thought all the female medics at his station were homicidal maniacs.

Maryellen let go of my shirt and playfully told me she had to go, pointing with her beautiful blue eyes to Lieutenant Lewis.

"Okay," I said, not even trying to hide my smirk. I glanced over at Sandra Sue on the passenger's side. She was stroking her hair. Sandra had a habit of doing that when she got aroused...trust me on that one.

"See you soon, I hope," Maryellen said before she drove away into the sweltering NYC summer night.

"What was that all about?" Bobby approached me as I walked back to my ambulance.

I told him she was in my academy class, and that was like a secret handshake all the cadets had. In disbelief, he stopped and stared at me as I took a few steps. "Bullshit!" He exclaimed, catching up with me.

By the time we finished decontaminating the ambulance, there was no one left in the parking lot. Tired and wet, we headed to the locker room, changed, and headed home.

CHAPTER FOURTEEN

Laundry Day

This happened few weeks after the merger with the NYC Fire Department and the Emergency Medical Service. Most of us were still confused because, if anything, we should have merged with the NYC Police Department. After all, we responded tandem on most 911 calls. But as Mongo in the movie Blazing Saddles would say, "We are just pawns in the game of life."

During that time, personnel was shifted to different battalions. The FDNY Chiefs changed unit call numbers, and Stations were now called Battalions.

We had a new insignia, and our uniforms had changed from green to blue and carried the FDNY patch. There were also new rules. It was almost like when you were a kid, and your family moved, and you switched schools. Now you had to make new friends.

After working for five days straight, I was told to come in for an overtime tour on my day off, which I wasn't pleased about, but everyone at the time had to do it because we are short-staffed. It was an easy 9 a.m. to 5 p.m. shift close to Cambria Heights General, and it was with my old partner Jimmy Kegan from a few years back. Jimmy was Irish and about my age—37 or so—and he drank about as much as I did, so we always got along.

That morning I pulled into the parking grounds like I always did, just minutes before my shift started and. As if to my mood, I began complaining how the job sucks. I walked out of the car towards the battalion to get my radio and quick-change into my blue FDNY uniform, I said hello to the desk lieutenant to prove that a real, breathing body was present to cover a vacancy on a unit.

As I walked over to where Jimmy was sitting on the ambulance drivers' side, I gave him a high-five, told him my shield number, and asked him to log us onto the ambulance computer. I told him to give me the extra key for the ambulance so I could throw my trauma bag inside.

"Do we have all the equipment on the bus?"

"I guess so," he replied.

That was good enough for me, so I threw my trauma bag into the side of the ambulance, jumped in the passenger seat, and said to Jimmy, "So how the fuck are you today?"

"Swell." He groaned at me with a hungover look.

About thirty seconds later, the dispatcher, seeing that our unit was in service, asked us to pick up a confirmed Shots Fired/Possible Injuries six blocks away from our location at Cambria Heights General (CHG.) Dispatch mentioned for us to wait for NYPD before entering.

Jimmy acknowledged with a "10-4."

"You ready?" He looked at me like he just got the green flag at the Indianapolis 500.

"Ready as I'll ever be." I laughed.

Jimmy took off in the ambulance with the lights and sirens blazing, scaring all the cats on the hospital grounds; the cat lady complained to the desk lieutenant a week later. As we pulled out onto the boulevard, I asked Jimmy if he had his vest.

"No, do you?"

"Nope."

"So, this is gonna be like a suicide mission?" He continued.

"I guess so." I shook my head.

About two minutes later, we showed up at the address we were given for the confirmed shots fired and saw an Asian lady standing outside a laundromat, screaming madly and pointing to her store. Next, I recognized the sound of a "pop." Definitely a gunshot. It's freaking 9:15 in the morning, and people are still shooting at each other like in the night shift? I stepped outside of our vehicle. This is not right.

Jimmy grabbed the Asian lady and got her out of the way of whoever was shooting. NYPD wasn't on scene yet, so we were the chosen ones at this point.

Jimmy moved her to my side of the ambulance, and we crouched down a little, so we were pretty much out of the line of fire. Jimmy then asked the Asian lady loudly, "What's going on?" But without understanding Cantonese or Mandarin, we were clear out of luck what this screaming lady was saying.

Another minute later, an NYPD cruiser showed up, and both rookie patrol officers got out and pulled their pistols. Jimmy and I made the universal sign for a gun with our hands and pointed at the laundromat.

I stood there watching the officers walk inside like they were ready to go into some gun battle at the OK Corral and thought to myself, maybe today was not a good day not to take my bulletproof vest.

About a minute later, I heard the radio dispatcher notify all NYPD units responding to slow it down. Apparently, one of the officers inside the laundromat saw that the coast was clear.

That was a relief.

A few minutes later, both officers came out of the establishment and walked towards us.

"What's going on?" One of them asked.

"Well, somebody fired a shot when we pulled up," I said.

"I heard it too. It was definitely a gunshot," Jimmy confirmed. "Is there anybody injured or shot inside?"

One officer looked at me and said, "There is a dead dryer inside."

"What?" I tilted my head.

The other officer told me to go inside and take a look. "It's all clear," he added.

I walked inside the laundromat and immediately smelled gun powder. That confirmed my suspicion that a shot was fired inside. I walked over to the dead dryer and saw that the glass window was shattered. Honestly, it looked like somebody had shot a round into the dryer. I scanned the place but didn't see any victims laying or sitting, for that matter. I walked outside again as the officers were trying to communicate with the Asian lady.

"What's up?" Jimmy asked.

I told him to go inside and check it out himself.

The NYPD supervisor showed up a few minutes later. I could tell he was not in a good mood because he sighed as he adjusted his gun belt when he got out of the car.

"What's going on?" He walked over to us and asked the officers trying to talk to the Asian lady.

"We don't really know; the lady doesn't speak English, and nobody knows what she is saying," the officer answered.

Hands on his hips, the sergeant turned around, looked at the sky while pulling out his portable radio, and asked the police dispatcher if unit 74-Victor was available. She told them they were on a 63 (Meal.) He told the dispatcher to pull them off the meal and have them respond ASAP to our location.

"Is she okay?" He then walked over to me.

"She looks fine to me," I replied.

I got into the back of the bus with the Asian lady and pointed to the seat, telling her to sit. Five minutes later, NYPD unit 74-Victor showed up. Two Asian American officers got out. The sergeant explained what we knew and told the officer to translate what this lady was talking about.

The officer sprinted over and got in the back of the ambulance with the lady and me. A few minutes later, the sergeant walked over to us, stuck his head in the back of the ambulance, and said, "Well?"

"Lady said man drop off laundry last night. He drops off every week; he is a policeman," the translating officer informed him.

"Wonderful" The sergeant looked at us. "What's his name?"

"She said it's on the laundry ticket inside. She said she does all drop-off laundry in the morning before the store opens." The officer asked the Asian lady and reported the translation.

"That's nice!" The sergeant blurted sarcastically. He then told the translating officer to tell the old lady that we were all going into the laundromat, and she had to show us the laundry ticket.

"I'll be here," I informed the police officers, who followed the store owner inside.

"Central is sending a boss over. We've been on the

job too long." Jimmy approached me.

A few minutes later, the Asian lady, Officer Chan—I learned his name only after reading his name tag—and the sergeant walked out of the laundromat. I could see the sergeant reading the name on the ticket. He knew exactly who this person was, and he just happened to be at work that day. His unit was available, and he was in the area. The sergeant got on the portable radio. "17 Frank, 85 me. No emergency."

The sergeant went back into the laundromat and came back out with a tattered NYPD shirt. At that point, NYPD unit 17 Frank had just pulled up. I'm not sure what was actually said, but one could tell somebody on 17 Frank just got yelled at, severely.

"Mark this 90, police matter only on your side. This is a police issue." The sergeant walked back to Jimmy and me.

We got his shield number and told our dispatcher to cancel our boss because our unit was back in service.

A few hours later, in our tour, we decided to take a swing by the police precinct and see if we could casually bump into the two officers we did the laundromat job with. Jimmy recognized one of them. We got out of the ambulance and walked over. Once he saw us, the officer started to chuckle.

"What was that all about?" Jimmy asked the officer.

Apparently, an officer who worked in the precinct had left a few rounds in his pocket after going to the range. He forgot about them when he dropped off his laundry. The Asian lady put his shirt in the dryer, and the rounds went off.

"No fucking way!"

"Yes, fucking way!" He laughed. "After the sergeant ripped him a new asshole, he had the translating officer tell the old lady that the nitwit who left the rounds in his pocket was paying for all the damage and a NEW dryer!"

"Wow!" We all laughed.

"You're lucky there weren't any moms with their infants doing the wash at the time. You could have little babies' brains all over the floor. And you know whose fault that would be!" The officer mimicked the sergeant screaming.

"Yikes!" Jimmy added.

"I don't think he is ever going to drop off his laundry. Ever!" He chuckled.

CHAPTER FIFTEEN

Next few years: 1997-1998

For the next few years, my life ran almost exclusively on autopilot. The 911 calls all seemed to be the same. It was a shooting, a stabbing, an injury, or a cardiac arrest. Then one day, after about fifteen years of doing this job, I was actually hoping for the cardiac arrest jobs.

It was almost like someone clicked the light switch in my head as I remembered when I first started in 1985. Back then, I actually got scared when I responded to cardiac arrest jobs; now, my whole demeanor had changed. It's just another call.

We'd brought quite a few patients back from the dead, but on the other hand, quite a few people had died in my arms. The asthma patients got to me, and that became my job of choice. I knew if we could get there, we could make a difference and save those people. If we showed up and gave them a treatment with oxygen and some medication, things would work out—especially with the adolescents.

***

The year was 1998. As soon as I walked into a bar, the sound of a tambourine attracted my attention. That wasn't the only lovely thing that was happening on that corner. The young woman playing it was attractive as well. Very attractive. So much so, in fact, that I put in a quarter in that musical instrument and made eye contact with her. It was love at first sight. Jeanne became my girlfriend and later my wife.

THE PHYSICAL TO BECOME AN NYC FIREFIGHTER, MARCH 2000

"**A**ll right, I passed!" The recruit, a young man approximately twenty-five years old, pounded his chest—his version of Tarzan.

The howling scream he made was sort of funny because he didn't sound like Tarzan at all, but it came from his heart. He finished his victory lap on the far side of the gymnasium, and I had to yell at him to come over to my desk, so I could take his vital signs one more time. Then he could go over to the bench and get further instructions. I couldn't help but smile at this kid.

He was so happy! Hell, I was happy for him!

At forty years old, I was aware of how hard this FDNY physical was. For six months, I'd watched regular kids come off the street and try to become an NYC firefighter. I knew most of them had a chance as long as they weren't too overweight or over twenty-five years old; that was my personal cutoff date. Sure, many people in their late twenties who were in shape passed, but in general, it was tough to pass without practice or working out.

I'm not sure about now, but the FDNY physical consisted of six different obstacles and tasks back then. It began with the Stairmaster. Then the candidate had to put up a ladder approximately thirty feet long. Another was an obstacle course that required crawling through a maze while dragging a dummy. Then the sledgehammer, the hose pulls, and finally the ceiling push, followed by pulling eighty pounds down on a sort of pneumatic pulley device.

It looks simple, but it's not easy.

One day I decided to try and take the physical myself, just to see if I still had it. After two minutes, I almost passed out on the Stairmaster, where one had to do at least fifty-nine steps a minute with fifty pounds on for five minutes. That was an awakening moment.

I really thought it would be a piece of cake. It wasn't.

My job was to help those who passed out while doing the physical. Luckily in those six months, nobody died, but quite a few did pass out. One guy thought he was going to die, and one didn't even want to go home after he failed the test; he was so heartbroken.

Among all the applicants, I met Mike, a fellow EMT who always wanted to be a firefighter. I'd worked with him for the best part of the previous year, 1999. For months he trained on how to tie various knots, as they were part of the test as well, just not in this stage. I learned some of it as well, along with him. I remember his confident look when he passed the finish line of that test. *I got this.*

On a beautiful hot July day in 1999, Mike and I were assigned to cover the JFK airport area. My dad took me to LaGuardia Airport when I was a kid, and together we watched the airplanes. Even at an early age, I liked watching the planes take off and land.

I knew that the Concord took off from Kennedy Airport, and lo and behold, the rumbling engine sound reached us. Mike and I walked over to the fence separating the end of Runway 42R from the service road. Mike, practicing his knots for the firefighter exam, had a few of the ropes in his hand. We could both see the pilot turning the plane to line up his take-off in the middle of the runway.

As we stood there with our hands on the wire fence, we watched as the pilot of the plane revved up its engines. I felt the hot air being pushed thru the SST engines as it took off. The air wasn't sweltering. It was more warm-like, but when the pilot gunned the engines, we felt it and decided, "Well, maybe we are a little bit too close." We scrambled back, releasing our grip on the fence to go stand behind the back of the ambulance.

We watched the Concord pick up speed, and about halfway down the runway, it ascended into the sky. It was indeed a sight to be seen. Modern technology at its finest; the Wright brothers would have been proud of how far their achievement had progressed over the years.

"You know if I wasn't going to be a firefighter, I would have wanted to be a pilot," Mike said as the aircraft passed us.

"I thought you were afraid to fly."

"Not me." He grinned.

We continued to watch the gracefulness of the plane as it made its left turn into the horizon and aimed towards the Atlantic.

"So, you want to be a pilot, but you would rather be a firefighter," I asked.

"I know it sounds crazy, but I think I was born to be a firefighter. I sort of have no choice in the matter.

But if I had, I would love to be a pilot." He wrestled with his reply.

We both hopped in the ambulance, I put the vehicle in drive, and we left the restricted area we were parked in.

Mike and I got along for the next few weeks, which was pretty rare, I might add, especially because I was a pain in the ass at times. Mike enjoyed helping people. It reminded me of why I got into this whole profession in the first place.

Sometimes when I look back at all the death and destruction on September 11, 2001, I keep thinking of the last thing I said to Mike.

"Make sure you keep your head up and look out for that falling debris...always look up!"

"Don't worry about it, Rocky. You just be careful out there too, brother," he replied.

CHAPTER SIXTEEN

September 11, 2001

My phone rang at precisely 0902 hours. I know because I looked at the nightstand clock as I picked it up.

"Quick, put on the TV! A plane crashed into the World Trade Center!" Barbara, my girlfriend's and my future wife's sister, who lived in Florida, screamed on the phone.

As I stumbled out of bed and walked over to the living room, I turned the TV on. My head in a haze, I stared at the surreal images on the screen. I remembered Jeanne's sister was still on the phone, so I walked over to the bedroom and woke Jeanne up.

"Jeanne, it's your sister on the phone. Wake up, sweetie," I whispered into her ear.

Jeanne rubbed her eyes. "What's going on?"

"I don't know. I'm still trying to figure it out. I think the World Trade Center is on fire or something." I gave Jeanne the phone so she could talk to her sister and resumed watching TV, trying to figure out what the hell was going on. That's when the reporter said that an airplane had crashed into one of the World Trade Center buildings.

"Holy shit!" I sat on the couch and braced myself. Grabbing the remote again, I channel surfed only to find out that all the other news channels displayed the same images and news. *This is really happening. OK, now what?*

Because I worked the night shift, my workday hadn't started yet. I would sleep till late at times to prepare myself for a possible double shift.

For the next hour or so, I watched the events unfold on the TV. At times I saw some of my co-workers, covered in soot, running for their lives. I saw one of my partners, Paul from Saint Vincent's Hospital in NYC, with his ambulance doors wide open and about a dozen patients exiting the vehicle. I then saw him make a U-Turn and head back toward the WORLD TRADE CENTER.

It was at this time I saw the bone-chilling collapse of the South Tower, live, on CNN.

I knew at this point it was going to be a very long day. I told Jeanne that I was going to take a shower and head up to the Battalion.

She was still on the phone with her sister when I came out of the bathroom. That's when I saw the North Tower Collapse.

My mind at the time was scrambling for items I might need, so I opened my knapsack and started throwing in whatever I could find, my cell phone with an adapter, binoculars, multitool, etc. I was glued to the TV set until the following scrolled on the chyron: ALL NYC NYPD FIREFIGHTER AND EMERGENCY MEDICAL PERSONNEL PLEASE RE-PORT TO YOUR COMMANDS.

The clock hanging on my living room wall read 11:15 a.m.

God help us all.

"Don't worry about all this. You just be careful," I told Jeanne as I grabbed my backpack and ran out the door, knowing this day was not going to be easy.

The drive to the Battalion building was almost on autopilot. My eyes were focused on the street, but my mind was a thousand miles away. *Was it a chemical cloud that I saw on TV? How many people are dead? Why is this happening? Am I going to die? Are my friends okay?*

The first thing I noticed at 1118 hours when I arrived in the parking lot of my station was the incredible amount of personnel. I didn't recognize most of them. The second thing I saw was there were no ambulances in the lot. That reminded me of the blizzard of 1994 when we were unable to get to work. We were told to get to the closest station. From there, we would find some way to go to our appropriate commands.

The mood inside the station was gloomy. From the rookies to the captain, no one knew exactly what was going on. A lot of bosses didn't want to give out any news until it was confirmed multiple times. That's when field personnel started passing the word around via radio. At first, it was stuff like, "Did anyone see my partner? We got split up when Tower Two came down. Was so-and-so working today?"

Rumors of multiple missing-in-action friends and coworkers ensued. Then specific names began to trickle in from various units who were down there. My head was on a swivel, and at times I would stop breathing while listening to the radio transmissions. I knew all of them. *The chaplain is DOA?* My God.

It's impossible!

The list just got longer and longer.

No one could substantiate or confirm any fatalities of the members of the service (MOS), but by this time, the phone calls were pouring in from worried family members. We had no confirmed information about the MIA's, just rumors. Just because someone wasn't picking up their phone didn't mean they were dead. Besides, the phone lines began to play games with us. Some lines were utterly unusable. I took at least ten phone calls that day. I remember telling the people on the other line that their loved ones were okay.

I lied. I didn't know where they were. No one did at the time.

Moments later, the TV showed ambulances and command cars crushed by rubble and fire trucks with open compartments littered with debris, some smashed to bits.

Most of us at the station would have loved to race down to the site, but at this time, there were no vehicles for us to use. To make matters worse, all the major highways and parkways were at a standstill.

After getting a little overwhelmed by all the television reports and the constant radio transmissions, I stepped outside for a minute. Henry Dee, one of my old partners, pulled into the parking lot at about this time. A bandana on his head covered a scar left from brain surgery he had a few months earlier. I quickly ran up to his car as he was parking. Maybe he had some news.

"Hey Dee, you see or hear anything from any of our bosses?"

"I just heard what was going on, and I jumped into my car and raced down here." Dee lived in Long Island, about thirty minutes away from the station.

"Where are all the cars?" Dee looked around.

"All over downtown Manhattan, or crushed, according to the CNN reports."

"You know they can't find my buddy Papageo." He echoed the voice of the worried family members who were calling the command.

"I didn't hear that name yet through the wires. Where does he work?"

"He just switched over to become a firefighter a few months ago, along with Kieffer and Gayner," Dee explained.

"There is so much confusion right now," I replied. "I don't know where he is."

"Do you think we can grab something to get up there?" Dee looked around the lot.

"Let's go upstairs and find out what plan 'B' is."

As we went upstairs to the supervisor's offices, a captain I had never seen before was sitting at the chief's desk.

"Hey Captain. What's up?" I greeted him.

"How are you guys doing?" He raised his head, greeting us. "I'm trying to get a ride to Manhattan." He directed his attention to the computer terminal on the desk. "You guys got any extra command cars?" he continued. "I don't see any cars in the parking lot in front."

"There's nothing out there," I said.

"But we do have a truck," Dee mentioned.

"That's cool. Standby, I might need a ride to the airport. Looks like Kennedy's flights have all been grounded." The captain got on the phone.

"Who the hell is that?" I asked Dee as we walked out of the office.

"I have no idea," he said. We left the captain talking on his phone and went down to the parking lot to have a smoke.

"I want to take the truck and go." I pointed to the smoke billowing from lower Manhattan where the twin towers once stood.

"Sounds good to me," Dee agreed.

At about this time, a semi-trailer rolled up to the

back of the morgue, adjacent to our station. I noticed the refrigeration unit attached to it. "Oh shit, I think I know what that's for!"

"What is that?" Dee looked confused.

"They're refrigerated trucks to hold the DOA's. I've seen them before," I said.

"That is NOT a good sign." Dee took a long drag on his cigarette.

***

Around 1300 hours, Dee and I finally decided that we should start dropping off equipment and personnel at different stations. Another supervisor asked us to drop off personnel at the Woodhull station in Brooklyn.

So, we left.

We got on the box truck, and I turned the radio on. I immediately recognized Moussa Diaz giving an interview, looking for his partner Paul Adams.

"I'm looking for my partner! The last time I saw him was down where the collapse was. The guy has no freaking fear...did you see him?"

After we loaded the truck with supplies, a few medics asked to get in the back. They squeezed in.

The ramp to Grand Central Parkway was blocked by a police car and a sign that read "ONLY emergency medical personnel." He let us in as we were in a marked FDNY truck.

"I remember the dust...that choking feeling...I took off my helmet and put it over my face, then me and this FBI agent grabbed onto each other and stood up against the wall of some building as close as we could, then we watched the North Tower collapsed at 10:29. MY DAMN WATCH STOPPED AT THE TIME OF THE COLLAPSE!" Paul Adams's voice came through the cabin speakers in another interview.

To say the drive was eerie was an understatement. I knew that what had happened was the biggest tragedy to hit this country since Pearl Harbor. I'll never forget driving on the Expressways. They were empty except for firetrucks responding from out in Long Island and police cars racing towards the plumes of smoke coming from Manhattan. When we got as close as the Brooklyn Bridge, I saw what looked like a giant movie set for a disaster movie. It was really creepy.

I wanted to continue past the Brooklyn Bridge into the city, but Dee thought it was better for us to continue with our original assignment: get equipment to the other stations. At this point, we were told the operation was in stabilization mode. The city of Manhattan was in lockdown.

Holy shit! A pair of F-16's roared above us. It was then when I realized that the typical New York sound—you know, airplanes flying overhead every few minutes or so—had vanished.

We briefly stopped at the Woodhull station, where I ran into one of my partners from the early nineties. It was then when I heard the station's supervisor address Dee regarding his hat.

"Is that Fire Department issued? If not, take it off!"

"Don't you have anything more important to do right now than bust my balls?" Dee took it off and informed him that he had brain surgery a few months back. The lieutenant shook his head and walked away.

Reality struck again when the radio started reporting that a terrorist group from the Middle East had hijacked the planes and crashed them into the World Trade Center towers.

Again?

My mother had been in the north tower in 1993 when they were the target of another attack by a terrorist group from the Middle East. She'd walked down the emergency stairway from the 80th floor. She'd told me the stairs were all dark.

Upon reaching Woodhull station, Dee and I split up.

Covered from head to toe with light brownish dust, some of our coworkers began to trickle in. The first one I recognized was Lieutenant Piro, then Paul's partner Moussa. Most of them just sat down in the recreation room, pushed their chairs inches away from the TV, and watched in silence.

"Did anybody hear ANYTHING about Carlos yet?" I asked, hoping at least one of the newcomers from Manhattan would know.

"No," Lieutenant Piro answered without taking his eyes from the TV.

"What about Quinno?"

"Nothing yet," somebody whispered.

"SHIT!" Moussa exclaimed in frustration.

The bad news just kept getting worse. As everybody continued to watch the television, the desk lieutenant walked up to Dee and informed him that he was going to commandeer our truck because his bosses needed a vehicle. So, along with all equipment and personnel dropped off, we found ourselves stranded.

My phone rang. I figured it was Jeanne; it turned out it was Kyle, one of my work partners who had transferred to the Bronx a month ago.

"Go," I answered the cell.

"What's your twenty? Are you at the site?" Kyle asked.

"Nope, I'm stuck in Brooklyn. No bus, no nothing. The bosses even took our portable radios. Where are you?" I replied.

"They got me moving FDNY engines off the site," Kyle said with a buzzing sound in the background.

"Really? Holy shit!" I said, fearing that some of these firefighters weren't coming back to their trucks.

"Yeah, it's really fucked up down here, total clusterfuck. Nobody knows what to do, not to mention who is in charge!" Kyle said.

"You okay?" I asked.

"I'm fine. They redeployed me from the Bronx at two p.m. to the West Side Highway downtown, and then one of the cops asked us if anyone knew how to drive a Firetruck. I said, 'I do.' The next thing I know, I'm in a patrol car heading to ground zero. We got as far as we can go on the West Side Highway, then we got out and basically ran over to an NYPD boss twenty blocks away. The one cop tells the boss, huffing, and puffing, that I can drive a fire truck. The boss looked at me, freaking out at the carnage, and pointed to vacant, damaged FDNY engines with mud monsters walking all around and told me to move them 'somewhere, I don't care where just get them the fuck out of here, the trucks are blocking my egress.' So that's what I've been doing for the past five hours."

"Mud monsters?"

"Yeah, people and members of the service. Everyone is covered head to toe with this grey dust!"

I could tell Kyle was driving one of the rigs. He hit one of the horns and yelled an expletive at someone blocking his path.

"So, you're okay right?" Kyle asked.

"Yeah, I'm fine," I answered. "Our bosses are having a hard time trying to find MOS that have gone MIA. The last thing they need is the ones that are accounted for to go missing," I explained.

"Listen, stay in touch. I think I'm gonna be here for days," Kyle said, still with that buzzing sound in the background.

"Don't get killed!"

"I'll try not to," he said, ending the call.

I looked up as a captain passed by, telling us that he was going in the direction of Astoria hospital. That was in our general direction. He offered us a ride, along with six other EMS/FDNY personnel that he had to drop off at various EMS/FDNY Battalions.

I'll never forget we stopped at a traffic light in

Astoria. As we all watched, a woman wearing a black hijab laughed and performed some kind of dance while she pushed her laundry cart across the crosswalk, looking at our FDNY truck. A lot of thoughts stormed my head as comments flew in the cabin.

Finally, at midnight, we were dropped off by the captain at Battalion 50. We then told our boss on duty that another boss took/borrowed our vehicle in Brooklyn, which he really didn't care about considering what was going on at the moment. I went downstairs to decontaminate ambulances that came back from the World Trade Center site.

This went on for hours. September twelfth's daylight crept up, and little by little, I saw progress around the battalion. We were all shell-shocked; that was expected.

As more personnel started to get back from Manhattan, I noticed they all had one thing in common. They were covered from head to toe with that dust. Some stuck around but most, wanting to go home and take a shower from all that "death dust" that clung to their uniforms, left.

The supervisors who came back were on adrenalin rushes. I remember one of the chief's aides telling me, "Rocky, I swear to god you've never seen a fat man run so fast when those buildings started to collapse. I never thought it was humanly possible for me to outrun ANYONE!"

Another chief's aide was in the hospital with a broken wrist caused by falling debris when the second tower collapsed. When we heard that he was alive with only a broken wrist, one of the secretaries in the office said, "Just because his last name is Kats, I hope he knows that he doesn't have nine lives left."

And then the vehicles started coming back.

"Holy shit," I kept saying to myself. Each vehicle came back with dust trailing it as it pulled into the battalion. It was like a dust storm following all of them. Even with driving on the expressway at fifty-five miles per hour for ten miles or so, dust was still coming off the vehicles. Some guys had left their windows open during the towers' collapse; the whole INSIDE was covered. I'm talking about two to three inches of this crap.

Then the Mobile Emergency Response Vehicle, MERV, pulled in. Its EMS/FDNY operator dismounted and looked at the vehicle he just got out of. The inside, just like the other vehicles, was covered in dust; the equipment was all over the vehicle like someone had picked it up and shaken it violently. At first, we couldn't believe the damn thing made it back because it was supposed to be buried in the rubble; at least that's what we'd heard.

The first thing I did was tell its operator, who was one of my partners, Bobby, to call his wife IMMEDI-ATELY. I explained that I'd received a call from her earlier. After getting ahold of him on a different radio frequency earlier, I told his wife that he was okay, but she was still distraught.

As I stood outside looking at all the damage done to the vehicles, our guys started referencing the WORLD TRADE CENTER site as "Ground Zero."

I sat down on the MERV's entrance steps and prayed. Not that they'd find the MOS missing, but for their souls, because at this moment, I knew a lot of good people were not coming home. The only way to help, I was told by many years as a Catholic school student, was to pray.

"Now I lay me down to sleep, I pray the Lord my soul to keep. If I die before I wake, I pray the Lord my soul to take. Please bless my family and Jeanne and please watch out for all those souls that never left Ground Zero, and please watch over us all, and let us do your work without any help from the devil. Amen"

I've prayed since the age of eight. I still do it to this day.

CHAPTER SEVENTEEN

September 12th, 2001

For the next twenty-two hours, I decontaminated all the equipment and vehicles that came back from Ground Zero. More information came in, but it really wasn't good news at all. I went into work mode and just focused on what I was doing. Eventually, I went home and saw Jeanne for the first time since we were watching the TV in the early morning of September 11th. We kissed, and I sat down; she had dinner waiting for me. I ate and then I saw all the phone messages.

"Who the hell are they from?"

"It's people that are worried about you," Jeanne answered.

Are people worried about me? Hell, I'm fine. "Who called?"

Jeanne went down the list, from various family members to my personal physician.

"What did you say? Did you call them?"

She explained that most of the people who inquired called back again, and she gave them the news that I was okay.

"Good girl." At the moment, I wasn't in the mood to make twenty phone calls. All I was interested in right now was going to sleep. I knew I was supposed to be back at the station after a nap. After dinner, I sat on the couch, and Jeanne held me tight, and I pretty much passed out from exhaustion in her arms.

Sleeping wasn't a problem back then. I was so exhausted from all the information the brain was processing, it wasn't till later that we all started having problems sleeping.

Returning to the battalion was very subdued; as much as all of us tried to get into a normal routine, we just couldn't. We all changed in some way after September 11, 2001. Jim Falconry didn't smile and tell the newest joke he'd heard on the Howard Stern show like he had every day for the past eight years. Marcy, the prettiest girl in the station, didn't look her best, and believe me, she took pride in ensuring she was the hottest thing in a uniform. We'd all lost a piece of our souls to an extent. I know that's a hard word, but we all seemed spaced out.

A few people turned to religion. I'm one of them.

After my second tour of working eighteen-hour days, I remember pulling up at my apartment and trying to figure out which side of the street I could park on. I couldn't even figure out what day of the week it was. If I didn't get some REAL sleep, I wasn't going to be any good to anyone.

I gave up trying to figure out what day it was, went inside, and passed out on the couch.

I did get a ticket, in the end, a fifty-five dollar one! The good people at the DMV decided to give me a discount and only charged me fifteen dollars.

The next few days were pretty much a haze, and then the captains and lieutenants started asking for volunteers to work on their days off looking for survivors. Most, if not all of us, jumped at the chance to work down at Ground Zero.

My first day working down at the site was three days after the eleventh. That was the first time I saw the magnitude of what had happened. The scene is still fresh in my mind like it just happened yesterday; too horrendous to describe.

Putting this down on paper is very difficult. I must say that in between the gruesome task I had, I noticed the heroic acts of civilians and uniformed members of the service, which I'll never forget. From the construction worker who carried two acetylene tanks on his back down into the pit of fire to the bucket brigade that consisted of everyone who could at the very least pass a bucket of debris. To the constant monitoring of clergymen and clergywomen who came up to us and asked us if we were okay and handed us food. One could tell this was the first time that everyone on the site was working together.

This is what AMERICA is all about.

So many branches of the service were down there that day. I could tell by the acronyms on the backs of their windbreakers: FBI, CIA, NYPD, FDNY, AIR-FORCE, USMC, and US NAVY. It was not just us either; they came from all over the world: SWISS ARMY, MEXICAN POLICE even the FRENCH FOREIGN LEGION were there, to name a few.

We all had one goal: to find survivors.

The prospects didn't look good. But hope kept us all digging, looking, listening, and risking our lives to find someone alive, anyone. Even if the odds were a trillion to one, that was good enough for us all. Even the rescue dogs searched twenty-four hours a day, seven days a week in the coming months. We all just kept coming in shifts from all over the world. If any good came out of this, it was the teamwork that we all showed as human beings. It's just a shame a horrendous act like this had to happen before we could show each other what deep-down all of us had, and that is common decency and the desire to live and help a fellow human being. Neither black nor white nor choice of religions could be used to deter us that day from our goal, and what I witnessed was very comforting.

Still, at that moment, my mind was full of hatred toward those who'd committed this cowardly attack. There was nothing I wanted more than to drop a bomb on that country and blow them straight to hell.

There were about four people from the station who happened to be off on September 16th, 2001. We all decided to work on our day off. The only person I remember from everyone there was Miller; he ended up being my partner for the day. At the meeting point in NYC, by the piers on the side of West Side Highway, we were briefed by our assigned lieutenant, supervisor, for the day.

At around 0830, a medic arrived at the meeting point. Passing in front of us he went up to the commanding officer and informed him that he was going to Ground Zero.

"First of all, where's your uniform?" the EMS/FDNY captain on duty for this operation said to the medic, a former U.S Marine who was wearing a volunteer fire department bunker gear.

"Why do I need it? I'm going down there to look for my friend!" The medic replied.

"Well, then you're going down there on your own time. What the hell is a matter with you?" The Captain continued, "You come to work, and you don't even have the right uniform?" The captain raised his voice. "You've been doing this in Brooklyn as well!"

"You know what...fuck you! I'm going to Ground Zero! I'll get down there with or without your help!" the medic shouted back as he flipped the finger to the captain and walked away.

"Not for nothing, boss," I tried defending him. "I think one of his Marine scuba buddies is MIA."

"Yeah, well, a lot of my buddies are MIA too." The Captain walked away.

The next thing I knew, we were heading downtown in the back of an FDNY ambulance. I think we had about seven of us in the back compartment; it was very quiet. Personally, I had reservations at this point. Not that I was scared or anything. It was more like I didn't know what to expect this time around. Maybe hesitation is the word I was looking for. But then I glanced at the medics and EMTs around at the back of the ambulance. Fuck it, if they are going, so am I.

At this point, I felt a little better. The ambulance continued to speed up and slow down as we approached intersections, some completely blocked while others regulated by PD. The vehicle slowed and stopped at some point, and someone outside shouted, "open the fucking back doors!"

Another medic entered the rear cabin where we were sitting.

"The first thing you got to do when we get dropped off is getting a mask...a good one, not that paper shit mask they issue us!" He closed the back doors and sat on the floor as the ambulance resumed traveling.

After a few military checkpoints along the way on the West Side Highway, all personnel in the back of the ambulance were dropped off. We then had to walk another ten blocks to our destination along with our helmets, trauma bags, and other equipment. Before entering Ground Zero, we needed to go to one of the makeshift NYC Fire Department trailers to get radios. We then continued to our destination of Vesey/West Street. We met up with Lieutenant Figueroa; he gave us the orders not to "get lost or killed!" He wanted to know where everybody was, at all times.

"If you're going to go to the bathroom, I want to know about it!" He was dead serious.

He then escorted us inside a badly damaged building and told us to set up our gear. Eight of us were going to relieve the other crews that worked the night before. It was about 10 a.m., so the tour that worked was going on their fifteenth hour of nonstop work. As soon as we got set up, the lieutenant said, "Move out. We're going up to the front."

As we walked through the building, I couldn't help but notice all the medical supplies stacked up. I mean everything medical, equipment, and supply-wise, including boxes marked morphine, were just sitting in the corner. As much as morphine is a controlled substance/narcotic, this was a different situation. This wasn't a controlled environment.

Other items donated consisted of basically everything you possibly could need for an operation like this. It was like Home Depot or a Walmart had opened their doors and said, "take anything you need." A lot of the donated items had little notes attached.

"OUR LOVE IS WITH YOU," from Kansas City, Missouri, or "HOPE IS NEVER GONE," from Lexington, Kentucky, or "YOU'RE OUR REAL HEROES" from Tampa, Florida.

Supplies were scattered all over the place, although there was some order to it. All the hardware, like ladders and work gloves, were outside, while blankets and medicine were inside. Then I heard that there were even more supplies in the piers uptown.

As our little squad continued following our lieutenant, we went outside into the courtyard. There were so many people in uniform you thought you were at some sort of Emergency/Police convention.

Finally, we turned the corner, and we all got a view of the destruction. Here it was, right before our eyes. It was like looking through Hell's gates.

Holy shit. I stared. It took a few minutes before my brain processed the data coming in. "Holy shit!" I said out loud.

I saw two massive steel mountains. Smoke and fire were coming out from underneath the one on the right. I don't remember which one of the towers used to stand there. The air smelled like death, and strangely enough, incense. The low-air chirps from firefighters' tanks echoed. I could hear them all over, but I couldn't see any of them. The piercing sound of ongoing deconstruction persisted. A thick layer of grey dust covered everything as far as I could see. Nearly a thousand people were scattered over almost sixteen acres, still looking for a miracle.

The lieutenant informed us that he needed two volunteers to relieve the other crew up front at the site.

"Let's go." I nudged Miller.

We got into a vehicle resembling a makeshift golf cart called a "Gator," and we headed past checkpoints towards the pile. There were no clear paths where to drive. We had to improvise.

As we relieved the crew that just worked fifteen hours, I stood next to the vehicle in shock. I couldn't help but look at all the people working on these two massive steel piles. Christ, the people look like ants on an ant farm colony.

We approached the crew we were going to relieve. They didn't waste time, just gave us the breakdown of the situation. "One horn blast means standby, something's going to fall. Two blasts mean something large will likely collapse. When you hear that, drop what you're doing and run toward the water."

They didn't mean run toward the Hudson river; they meant to run toward where the potable water truck was. "That's where the safe area is."

The primary fear at the time was that the slurry wall holding the Hudson river was going to give in, and the river was going to flood the debris field.

"Right now, we are in charge of all the DOA's. Every time they find a body part, make sure it's tagged. It's supposed to say where they found it, and then after a while when it's not too busy, one of you take a ride over to the makeshift morgue and release them to the medical examiner on duty."

Before I knew it, a call came in: pick up a deceased member of the service, MOS.

For the next fifteen hours, first responders would drop off bags with body parts at our little tent, and our job was to make sure they were stored correctly. Ground Zero was enormous, beyond my worse nightmares. The whole area of our operation was deemed unstable, hence the warning rules we were briefed on.

Unstable? Who the fuck really cares at this point? Look at all these people working and searching. If they don't give a shit, why the hell should I?

The bucket brigade, hundreds if not thousands of people, passed debris from the two steel mountains. Sometimes they would pass a big piece of metal. Whatever the hell they were doing, I wanted to go down and help.

"What good am I? Watching over body parts. Let me go down and help!" I talked a lot to myself. One of the bosses heard me mumbling.

"No! Your job is to help *those* people." He pointed at the site. "Look around; if they fall, they're going to be hurt."

Dejected, I continued my work.

"EMS, over here!" A cry came over the radio.

One of the workers had fallen and broken his leg. So off we went to the location before our boss got on the radio and told us to stand fast and watch over the remains he was recovering. Another crew was going over to the patient with the broken leg.

A few minutes later, the crew treating the patient asked us via radio to get a longboard. On the way back to the scene, the crew passed me with the patient in the back of their Gator. Sighing, the longboard in my hand, I walked toward the crew that had finally come to a stop some hundred yards or so away at a makeshift triage center. One of my fellow coworkers started yelling at me that I wasn't doing my job.

Frustrated, I shouted back.

The Lieutenant heard the commotion and approached the two of us. "If anybody is going to be doing the yelling around here, it's gonna be me! Take a time-out," he instructed me.

Hungry, aggravated, and tired, I decided to take the "time-out." Before I could do that, though, a piece of glass came crashing down near us. Now we had to relocate our makeshift triage area.

Then patients started to come over to us, telling us they had something in their eyes. I treated one or two, and by this time, the medic I had the argument with was close enough to talk to.

"Do you still love me?"

She smiled. I mean, we weren't the best of friends throughout the tour, but at least we tolerated each other.

I walked back to where Miller, my partner for the day was and saw some other EMTs I hadn't seen in a while. A few of us hugged each other when we saw that we were alive, and a few told us some bad news about how they still hadn't found so-and-so or somebody's wife was missing.

Then I saw Stephen, the guy who'd yelled at the captain to "fuck-off." Dust covered him head to toe. He came up from the pit to get something to eat and drink.

"Boy, you really know how to piss off someone," I said. "Not that I'm any better."

He sighed. "I came down here to look for my buddy. I don't really give a shit if I get paid or not."

We both sat down for a moment. Stephen described what a great friend he had and how "he just might be dead." But that he wasn't giving up yet, because his friend wouldn't give up on him if he was missing. After a few minutes, he was on his way back down into the pit, and I was being paged to come back to the location where my partner was.

Upon arrival, I told Miller to take off and get something to eat. "I'll hold down the fort. Just listen to the radio. If I need you, I'll call you," I said as he walked away.

I stared at all the red and green bags on the ground. Each was filled separately with a piece of a bone or an arm or a leg. Whatever it was, it was human in origin. We got into a routine of waiting until we had a bunch of red and green bags before we left the scene and headed to the makeshift morgue.

That wasn't easy either. I mean, traveling in a golf cart along the makeshift paths between the mangled debris of Ground Zero, we both were concerned we would lose a bag, so we came to an agreement. My partner would drive, and I would watch the bags in the back to make sure we didn't lose any.

I remember a bag shifted and fell. We stopped and rushed to grab it. A bloody piece of a thigh slipped through, then an arm. I remember swallowing, kneeling, and placing everything back inside. That was once a person. A parent, grandparent, spouse. Someone's child.

I found myself sighing a lot. I guess that was one of my coping mechanisms. Then I recalled that, during the previous year, there had been a rash of suicides in the NYPD and EMS. A lot of those statistics were reaching the media. The politicians at City Hall had come up with a solution. All the first responders to take another class in "wellness." That would show that they, the politicians, were doing their job.

The course, called something like "Other ways to handle stress," was pathetic; we all had to fill out questionnaires and then sign them. After that, an instructor who had spent most of their career in a classroom and not in the streets gave us "hints" on ways to cope with stress and told us, "don't kill yourself," at the end.

I recall thinking that nothing I learned there helped.

Every time a member of the service, firefighter, EMT, or police officer was found, we would all stop. We would salute while the body was brought out of the pit on one of the Gators.

Later in the day, I ran into Lieutenant Bauer from my battalion. At first, I didn't recognize him; he looked like a mountain climber with all the ropes and gear he was wearing. I told him how glad I was that one of the good bosses was down here. He explained his job was to climb up the mountain of steel with his partner in case anybody got an injury.

The clergymen would frequently walk by everyone and check on them. "Are you okay, son? Is there anything I can get for you?"

"If one more freaking priest asks me how I am, I'm gonna start to think that there is something wrong with me," I told my partner after hearing this question about a dozen times.

"Get used to it." He faintly chuckled. The priests and all the spiritual advisors were asking the same of all the workers.

As the hours went by, I saw so many acts of heroism in the pit. I also remember a lot of crying.

I remember that one girl who just sat on the curb near Ground Zero with her head down and stared at the ground in front of her. Once in a while, she would pick her head up and look around. I walked over and asked her if she wanted a soda or something; she just sighed and refused with a polite, "no, thank you."

She sat on that curb for close to ten hours—didn't move from that sitting position. If anyone needed a priest, she did; I was already too far gone.

After the exchange with the lonely sitting girl, I resumed my walk. Because there were loose panels and beams everywhere, I had to look down and be mindful of my footing. Something caught my eye on the ground in front of me. As I bent down to take a closer look, I saw a WORLD TRADE CENTER Employee ID card. I knew what one looked like because my mother had worked in the WORLD TRADE CENTER in the eighties and nineties, and she had a WORLD TRADE CENTER Employees ID badge hanging in her den in Long Island.

My mother explained that she was in the first bombing at the WORLD TRADE CENTER in 1993. She said when the bomb went off, the whole tower shook and the lights went out, but what fascinated her was that all the phones worked. After climbing down thirty-seven floors in the dark and smoke-filled stairwell with everyone else, she emerged with her friend into the lobby and was greeted by dozens of FDNY/EMS/NYPD personnel. A triage tag was put around her neck, and she was told to wait in the lobby until EMS personnel could take a look at her and determine if she needed to be transported to the hospital.

Her first instinct had been to get as far away as possible from the WORLD TRADE CENTER. "I'm wasn't going to hang around in the lobby for another bomb to go off." She told me. Eventually, she'd made her way home. After that bombing incident, my mother decided to retire.

I looked at the name on the ID card. I just couldn't imagine my own mother in a carnage like this. I shuddered at the thought, picked up the card, and brought it over to the NYPD. The officer looked at it, then wrote the name down. He proceeded to toss the ID card in a big box filled with other World Trade Center ID cards. I couldn't help but think of all those poor lost souls. "Nothing left but an ID card."

As the sun started to set and the generators powering the lights turned on one after the other, Ground Zero took on a different look. All the volunteers were still in the middle, searching for any signs of life. The pace did not slow down. If anything, it got faster once the new crews set up to relieve the previous ones.

It was time for us to leave.

We backtracked the ten-block hike we'd taken when we first arrived. Dragging ourselves into the ambulance that dropped us off, all of us were emotionally drained. The adrenaline that we'd had at the beginning of this sixteen-hour tour had been wholly sucked from our bodies. All of us were mentally and physically exhausted. Once I sat down somewhere in the back of that bus, nothing in a million years could get me back up again.

As the ambulance drove up the West Side Highway, somebody opened the back doors. Each side of the highway was packed with people holding signs that read "WE LOVE YOU" and "YOU ARE HEROES." People were clapping like it was some sort of a parade or something when we drove by. The closer we got to the pier, the more people there were. I mean, people had strollers out, and the kids were holding signs.

"Do you see that?" I looked at my partner, pointing to everyone lining the street as we zipped by in the ambulance.

"Yep…. I told you we should've walked," he said, looking and waving at those kind people wishing us well.

"What, are you crazy? With all our equipment, lugging it ten blocks and then walking another two miles back to the pier? Remember we still have to make it back into Queens and then get to our cars and go home," I said, watching the people cheer and cracking a smile for the first time in a while.

"I guess you're right…besides, I'm starving." Miller and I both smiled at the people lining the streets as we passed them by.

We were all heroes in the back of that ambulance, and for a moment, I felt like one. But that didn't last long. We still had a lot more work to do; this was only the beginning. At this point, I looked out of the window. A bystander was holding a sign that read, "PLEASE DON'T LET THIS HAPPEN AGAIN."

I will never forget that sign. It was almost as if

time slowed down as we passed by it.

By the time I got home, it was close to midnight, and the first thing I did before I came into the apartment was to strip down outside in the hallway, totally naked. There was so much *death dust* all over me. The next thing I did was hightail it towards the shower to wash all of it away.

"Are you OK?" I asked my reflection in the mirror. "I guess I am, I hope," I answered in my head.

I couldn't help but notice that my right eye sclera, the white part, was completely red, so I flushed it out a few times. I then put my gym shorts on and collapsed on the couch. I knew Jeanne would be a little late, so I ended up channel surfing. All the stations had more information about the terrorist attacks on the WORLD TRADE CENTER and the Pentagon. Depressed, I shut it off and fell asleep.

We were lucky we were still here, and all our family members seemed intact and accounted for. My mother didn't take it too well at first because of her history in the first World Trade Center bombing. She knew a lot of the people who were missing and presumed dead. She broke down and cried every time the topic would come up. Which it did. A lot. "I feel so bad for those people."

I didn't exactly announce that I was working down

at Ground Zero, but most of my friends wanted to know what it was really like after a while. I wanted people to understand the carnage of what these terrorists did. So, at times I would be graphic. I remember a year later, the child psychologists started coming out of the woodwork telling all the parents of five- and six-year-old children not to let them watch the first-anniversary special. "They'll think it's happening again, and they'll grow up all fucked up." Professional people in the mental health department didn't even want teenagers to watch what really happened because it might deter them from their studies, and they might get all fucked up too.

What is going on here? Are we all in denial or something?

If it were up to me, I'd take every kid down to the site, from kindergarten to twelfth grade, as part of a class trip and explain to them that all those first responders died trying to save people. Heroic acts were performed by citizens who refuse to leave their fellow worker because he was stuck in a wheelchair, or by the young mother-to-be who had everything going for her but stayed with a dying coworker who asked her not to leave her side because she was trapped. It's all about us and how this disaster affected all of us, some for the good and some for the bad.

I want people to understand how many good

people were lost and that now it's time for all of us to take their place and become good people.

***

The Cantor Fitzgerald global financial services company employees memorial was held in Central Park on October 2nd, 2001. Paul and I were asked to attend by one of the bosses there.

Before I go any further, I would like to say "thank you" to all those who came up to us and either gave us a hug or offered condolences for our members lost on 9/11. Without those people, I don't think I would be writing this book. I know most writers get into what they are writing; in this case, what I got into, made me write this. Even if this goes into a folder that is tossed into a backroom closet or filed away in a stack of unused floppy disks, I still have closure from completing this.

As the years have gone by, my mind has been polluted by so many horrific encounters. One thing comes to my head when I think of them: Psalm 23:4 *Even though I walk through the darkest valley, I will fear no evil, for you are with me; your rod and your staff, they comfort me.*

I know we must all move forward in life. Still, I hope the citizens of this great country will never forget the atrocities that happen some 20 years ago as of the time of this publication, May we never see the monstrosity that occurred on September 11, 2001, again. Even as innocent children watched the Towers collapse, one can only think of the human life, which was so carelessly wasted.

Sometimes God doesn't even have the answers to the questions we all seek; that's why he gave us life, for our job is to find the answers and relay them back to him. We are his messengers, not his destroyers.

CENTRAL PARK, NYC, OCTOBER 2, 2001

A
s I stood at attention on a wooden pedestal in the background of the memorial service, I watched my friend Frank as he listened intensively to the priest speaking at the podium. Paul and I were Frank's guests. Even though this was not a memorial for an FDNY member, both Paul and I had decided to come in dress uniform.

For the first time, I attended a service for civilians killed when the World Trade Center Towers collapsed. I found out that over six hundred and fifty-eight people from the offices of Cantor Fitzgerald were killed. I took a deep breath, trying to visualize the company's enormous task in front of itself. As I gazed at the family members wandering around, I noticed little children with pictures of their mommy or daddy pinned to their clothes like badges of courage. Even the grownups had the pictures on.

From time to time, I noticed gusts of winds coming and going. A priest remarked about the winds and said it reminded him that the winds were the souls of those lost during the attack and that they were restless not for themselves but for their loved ones. It was a little spooky.

As time moved on, the winds subsided, and the threat of the tents crashing down on everyone seemed to disappear altogether. It was strange to be in a civilian setting where only my partner and I appeared to be the only people concerned about the possibility of a disaster. Hell, we already had an escape route and a possible triage area set up in our heads just in case a Multi Casualty Incident occurred. Sometimes I wish I didn't know about these things, but this is what we are trained to do, control the scene and get the injured out of harm's way, and like all MCI's, the art of improvisational life-saving techniques is the key to saving one's life. While everyone was grieving, including myself, the stress and horrors I witnessed in Ground Zero were still fresh in the back of my head.

Watching Frank with his daughter and niece, I couldn't help but wonder about his situation and how he felt as he watched the video monitor flash the faces of those lost. Frank was supposed to be at the Trade Center, but by chance, one of his daughters was caught intoxicated by her mother, and

Frank was told to come home and give her a lecture on the dos and don'ts of responsible drinking.

As I watched Frank, I realized we were all the same when it came to losing someone close. I remembered one of the first times I met Frank; he'd showed me a list of names on a legal white pad. Some had yellow highlights drawn across the name. I asked if those were the people who were MIA, and he told me, "No...those are the people alive."

Christ, there must have been fifty to a hundred names on a page, and he had a lot of pages. When he told me about the letters of condolences he was writing, I thought this guy must be an extraordinary individual to do this task almost by himself. Deep down, maybe we all have a hidden agenda that God only knows.

As the memorial ended and the politicians made their speeches, we left and walked over to the Carlyle Hotel for refreshments and a bite to eat. The hotel banquet room began to overflow, so Frank decided that we all should leave and go back to his hotel. Although it was only 5:30 p.m., he'd been up since 5 a.m. He told me that he started his day by walking downtown from 59th Street and Sixth Avenue to Ground Zero. The reason for that was he wanted to start the day like most of those who were lost had.

As we reached the New York Athletic Club, we stopped by the bar inside the hotel and had a few beers, toasting those who were lost and alive. With that, Frank and his family left.

Paul and I stayed and drank at the beautiful bar inside the NYAC, and both of us ended up narrating the two-hour special on 9/11. Quite a few members of the club had questions about what happened in Ground Zero.

As the special ended, we were congratulated for a job well done; there were many pats on the back and some photo ops. At this point, our dress uniform looked a little disheveled, so we both straightened out each other's ties before a picture was taken after all was done. Paul and I departed, and as the car sped into the night, we decided to move on and not look back. We both knew we could never forget what happened to us in the past year, but for some strange reason, we both agreed:

"That's what our brothers would have wanted."

CHAPTER EIGHTEEN

Back in the pit.

The date was October the eleventh, 2001. I was sitting in the makeshift golf cart, waiting for more bodies to be found. I was thinking back through the past eleven years in which I worked on and off with Carlos as a partner responding to 911 calls. Years have taken a toll on me more than him. I was still trying to figure out how I lost so much hair, yet Carlos still looked like Tom Selleck, the movie star.

Like any other day at Ground Zero, I was exhausted

from the smell of smoke, decomposing bodies, and asbestos. The elements of nature had turned the area into a horrific mountain of mangled and broken steel. The dirty, broken pieces of glass glowed and reflected the mostly grey surroundings at any given time of day. Paths made by the first responders were taking shape while the sound of chainsaws and other power tools occasionally broke the silence.

"We have to bring these guys home," Carlos's words pulled me out of my introspection. In a haze, I looked at him, then at everyone who was searching the ruins.

"They just found another one. I think it's one of us this time." Carlos pointed.

Next to a group of first responders, who were congregated into a semi-circle some three hundred yards below, a tired and beaten medic waved. That was the signal for us to go down and retrieve a body.

The drive itself was not a long one, but I was daydreaming into the past as Carlos slowly drove next to the volunteers and different governmental agencies.

"So, what the hell were you thinking about this time?" Carlos abruptly broke my concentration.

"Just drive and watch out for those freaking

craters." The mounds of dirt roads seemed to break away on each side.

"Look, Rocky, don't overthink; remember the academy. Let's just do our job and move on. We can't beat ourselves up about this; it's over. They're dead. What we have to do is keep sane and not lose sight of the objective!" Tight-lipped, I looked over at Carlos. I knew he was right. I just didn't want to accept it. "We're picking up another bag of bones, a human being basically cremated and crushed beyond recognition. It's fucking depressing. I just want it all to stop."

"Relax, brother Rocky; we're bringing them home." Carlos pitched in.

The sound of jackhammers pouncing with fury intensified as my mind drifted again. I thought about how Carlos and I got along so well for such a long time.

"Yeah, I guess you're right. We are taking them home, and that does mean a lot, doesn't it?" With a playful shot to the shoulder, we both cracked a brief smile. In this hellhole, a partner like Carlos could soothe my mental lapse, and for that, I'm grateful to this day. There was nobody I'd rather travel through that Hell with other than him.

We drove the body to the makeshift morgue tent then went back on our post. Waiting for the next signal for service.

***

The first two months were surreal. Crying was constant, but I only did so in private. My lost brothers' conversations remained part of a daily routine; sometimes, I had to pull over wherever I was and break down. I don't know what triggered the emotional outbursts. All I know is, thankfully, they all remained with me.

I thought that I was taking this too hard. Maybe I should speak to a psychiatrist. At times I visualized the towers collapsing on my brothers. Those days still reoccur in my dreams. Alcohol and my remaining friends mostly help deaden the pain; we all used each other for a crutch.

"We belong with the living, not the dead," was a big catchphrase that most people who hadn't been down at Ground Zero would say to me. I got so tired of it sometimes.

In the coming months, most of us returned to Ground Zero doing the same thing: looking for a miracle. Maybe we could still rescue someone. We would do twelve-hour tours which really lasted sixteen to eighteen hours.

The search was called off in late November 2001. *We are going into the "Recovery Phase" of the World Trade Center Multiple Casualty Incident.* That didn't sit well with any of us. We knew pretty much at this time everybody missing was gone; we all knew it deep down. After a month, somebody had to say it to us officially. That's when the nightmares ensued for all of us.

A lot of soul-searching for me went on during this time, but then it was time to go back to work on my regular unit, which really wasn't regular anymore. Once or twice a month, I would still go down to work in Ground Zero.

***

The day after Veterans Day 2001 was supposed to be one of those slow days. After all that had been going on, some people decided to take that extra day off to relax. Even Carnival Cruise Lines offered a free night on a "cruise to nowhere" for FDNY personnel and their family.

Some people took them up on this; other people decided to just stay home. I happened to be off that day, so I saw this when I put the TV on in the morning.

"FLIGHT 587 CRASHES IN BELLE HARBOR, QUEENS. NOVEMBER 12, 2001 - 260 SOULS PERISH."

That headline hit me like a sledgehammer. Once again, I braced and sat on the couch for a few minutes to digest what I was witnessing. Flashbacks ensued.

Here we go again.

I walked into the bedroom and woke my darling Jeanne to explain to her that another plane had crashed, this time in Queens. As we both sat on the couch watching all the videos coming in and the speculations of the newscasters, the phone rang. It was one of the medics who'd survived the World Trade Center collapse. Tower One had been falling and heading his way. He'd known he was dead meat—then suddenly, the building buckled. He was spared.

"Steve, did you see the reports?" He asked. I knew what his next question was going to be when he got the chance to ask it.

"Yes...a plane went down in the Rockaways," I answered. "I'm watching the news right now."

"Come on, let's go." Paul was going, no doubt about it.

Jeanne gave me a look while I was watching the live feed videos of the crash. I sensed she didn't want me to go.

"It doesn't seem we're needed there, Pauley." I heard nothing on the other side. "I think he left the phone off the hook," I told Jeanne, who said she was going to use the bathroom.

I heard the shower being turned on, so I called my battalion and spoke to Lieutenant Quines, and I asked him if I should come in.

"Nope, no survivors," he answered bluntly. "No need for more personnel. We still have a city to run."

As I sat down on the couch, the television showed clips of destruction on the ground from Chopper 7. I started thinking about the planes that hit the World Trade Center.

The rest of the day was pretty rough. "Just when you thought it was safe to get back into the water, what happens?" I said to myself, thinking of the movie Jaws.

I prayed that at this point, it wasn't another terrorist attack. It turned out the crash of Flight 587 was a coincidence, nothing to do with terrorism. It was lousy timing, but it was a cruel coincidence, nonetheless.

It's not like I wasn't going to see my share of gore from this incident. I knew that I was going down to the Rockaways the day after, so I prepared my knapsack with a radio, some tools, a flashlight, etc.

As the following day came, I realized I was off, so I didn't go to work. This had happened five times in my past ten years of service. Usually, I'd go in, and the desk lieutenant would tell me to go back home. "You're off, remember?" Believe me, I'm not the only one; sometimes, stress will do that to you as well.

Jeanne and I just stayed home and had some quality time with each other; neither of us remembered the last time we both were off at the same time.

After my day off, I reported to work and was assigned to head to the Rockaways with the Mobile Emergency Response Vehicle, MERV. The vehicle itself was the size of an NYC Transit bus. The inside had been refurbished to hold six or more patients along with medical equipment. Basically, one could perform surgery in there if one had to. The MERV had just come back from the Rockaways, and now it was my turn to operate this mobile operating room.

As I drove down Woodhaven Boulevard towards the Cross Bay Bridge, I pulled over to a bodega. I got the feeling that the rest of my tour would be basically sitting in the vehicle, so I got a sandwich and a few sodas for myself.

I exited the bodega and drove down Cross Bay Boulevard past a gas station. A plane engine was sitting smack in the middle of it. Holy shit, it just missed the pumps. Thank God the plane didn't crash into the gas station.

Upon arrival at the crash site of Flight 587, I noticed the destruction. "Not again."

I approached the scene. About five blocks were blown away. Swept by the crashing aircraft. I could see the plane's glide path as it had slammed through the trees and crashed into houses. I parked the vehicle and went outside to report to the C.O, then momentarily stood and looked at the whole scene.

It doesn't look that bad.

The tragedy was that, in my head, I was comparing this airplane crash to Ground Zero. Little did I know that this accident was the second-worse in aviation history in the U.S.A. Flight 800, which had crashed off Long Island in the summer of 1996, was the worst. I remembered that day because my partner Betty Jacobs, a very religious woman, and I had been taking a break on Union Turnpike eating a slice of pizza when a message came over the computer that there was a plane crash in eastern Long Island. It was possible that we would have to respond. I think it was about forty-five minutes later the tour commander decided that sending units seventy-five miles out to Long Island just wasn't in the cards. There were plenty of volunteer ambulances. The debris area was seven to ten miles out at sea.

As I walked in the general direction of the command center, I saw the temporary morgue tent. It was about this time I noticed a car in a garage connected to a completely wiped out house. I peered inside and saw it was a Toyota. I assumed that occupants of that house were not around anymore.

The rest of the work tour consisted of helping some of the other units pick up body parts—Bag and Tag. I again compared it to my experience in Ground Zero and thought there really wasn't too much clean-up. NYC FDNY/EMS were getting really good at ensuring the remains weren't in public view for long. In forty-eight hours or so, all the bodies were removed.

This past year had been a nightmare for everyone on this job! Too bad the city of New York didn't realize how lucky they were to have these highly trained professionals at their doorstep a few minutes after one would dial 911.

The following days I spent making sure the MERV was in running order and that everybody had shelter. It was cold outside, so I made sure the heat was blasting in the vehicle. A lot of cops who were posted outside on the ghoul detail came in to warm up as well. They were making sure nobody stole anything.

Yes...unfortunately, people still rob the dead, I'm sorry to say.

As the day went into the night, lights came on with the generators provided by out-of-state construction companies. All of ours were down at Ground Zero. I walked over to the Red Cross tent to get a bite to eat, and some kid from upstate NY asked me if I could sign his jacket. I looked at him funny; he then explained that he worked down at Ground Zero, and he thought that all the members of the FDNY were heroes. He was going to save the jacket once he got home and never wear it again.

Boy, this kid has a lot of signatures on this jacket. I obliged and signed it.

The next few days weren't that bad for me personally. For once, my relief showed up on time regularly, and for that, I was grateful. The whole time I was down at the crash site of 587, everyone working was comparing this disaster site to Ground Zero and saying how the crash site wasn't a big deal compared to it. It was a mistake I caught myself making when I first walked into that site. How the hell could anybody say the loss of two hundred and sixty souls wasn't a big deal? I think it was two hundred and sixty-five; five people on the ground were killed.

The one thing that really struck me was the bar/restaurant across the street. I just kept picturing that if this plane accident had happened, let's say around on happy hour or on a Friday or Saturday night, many more people on the ground would be dead. After three days, all the politicians started coming down to the site and making speeches. I saw Mayor Giuliani again and Governor Pataki. At one point, I stopped to chat with some highway police officers in charge of the motorcade. Every once in a while, someone would call out that they found another body part, but at this point, we were completely desensitized to the view and smell. We just bagged and tagged it.

CHAPTER NINETEEN

Christmas Eve, 2001

I grabbed a beer while watching my obliviously happy nephews and nieces opening gifts while in my uncle's house in Long Island. Everyone tried their best to distract me from what I was going through, but the kids were the icing on the proverbial cake. I couldn't help but think that I was lucky to be in a situation like this. Though my family members asked me all the time what it was like working in Ground Zero, I seldom responded. I walked into the TV room, and Carlos Lopez's voice shook me.

"Yes, I know it's depressing being down at Ground

Zero on a Christmas Eve, but maybe we can bring someone home."

***

Days turned to months, my job and life continued. At this point, I had stopped recording my life as I used to. Most of my notes became events and names of coworkers I lost in Ground Zero.

***

9/1/2002, and here I am, back at Ground Zero for another round of Let's see how much I can take.

After attending roll call at the pier like the last time, I found out that one of my partners for the day was Mark Shift from my Battalion. "Boy, it's been how long since we saw each other? Eight hours? Nice to see you, Mark!" I walked over to him as we continued to say hello to other old faces we hadn't seen in a while.

Every time we saw a fellow coworker down at the WORLD TRADE CENTER, it was like we hadn't seen them in years, or we were just glad to see that they were alive, not just me, but everyone else too. Unlike the NYPD, which at the time had about 38,000 officers in the force, the FDNY/EMS was a pretty tight community with only about 3,000 of us. At this point of my career, in over ten years of working for the service, most of us had seen each other once or twice in our travels. So, a catastrophe like this was like a reunion of sorts. We used to meet at parties or outdoor events like a baseball game, but ever since we'd merged with the FDNY, we'd been kind of looked at like the stepchildren. Not that we really gave a shit; it was all politics. In the end, all I cared about was getting a check for doing my job just like everyone else.

Upon arrival, I noticed a big difference in the cleanup. Most of the rubble had been removed, and I could actually see the foundation and the subway tubes on the east side of the site. The cranes could move around a lot easier, and there now was a big ramp for the trucks going in and out. The last time I had been here, there was no defined ramp. But the steel mountains still persisted. I tried not to look too long. I didn't want to get caught up in comparing every little thing to the last time I was here.

The lieutenant who was in charge happened to be from Queens, and he knew Mark. He assigned us to do the important detail: working inside the Morgue tent.

Great, more fucking nightmares.

Mark and I were assigned to keep track of all the body parts, as well as possibly make an ID on some of the remains that were coming in. Of course, we had help; we were just the guys who did the paperwork and sometimes helped to search through the remains. Activated in the event of a disaster, the real heroes in this department were the Disaster Mortuary Operation Response Team members, DMORT.

At first, we introduced ourselves to the medical examiner, the M.E, who happened to be from Queens General. A really helpful fella. I remember he asked me if I was okay a few times. "You're doing a great job."

I remember mumbling "whatever" in a haze.

Mark was great; he made sure all the paperwork up front was in order. Two priests were assigned to the morgue tent, and they were also very helpful, especially when remains came in four to five at a time. At this point, things started rolling at a fast pace.

My job was to log all the remains that came in those red and green bags. *Now I know what happened to the bags after we brought them in the last time I was working in Ground Zero.* They were opened, and the M.E and her crew would try to decipher what part of the body it was. At times a whole body would come in. What really sucked was when they brought in remains with FDNY bunker gear or an NYPD gun belt that we recognized.

For some reason, they found a lot of deceased fire-fighters and police officers that day, and sadly we had to log them in the book.

LOCATION: where the remains were found.

AGENCY: what kind of uniform did they have on.

IDENTIFICATION: did the remains have a name-plate or a shield

ITEMS: what they had in their pockets

There were so many. I remember the M.E asking me to help them out. Some of the doctors were having problems identifying if it was one of our people, meaning FDNY. They knew that I worked for FDNY, so they asked me to look at the remains and possibly find a name somewhere.

At times the remains were so far gone that we couldn't make out anything. With others we did make out their name, usually from the helmet they were wearing. Often, a photo of a family member would be in there; even with the con-dition of the remains, the picture would remain intact. This went on for a while, then the priest would say a prayer. I swear I thought I was going to break down every time he read it.

When we finished doing what we were supposed to do, the body was draped in an American flag.

A few firefighters came into the tent when summoned, and they took the stretcher with the remains uptown to the Chief Medical Examiner's office on First Avenue.

I remember another medical examiner from Texas yelling at the firefighters taking out the remains, "Stars first!"

At first, I had no idea what that meant since I was never in the military, but a few people knew what she was talking about. We had to turn the stretcher around, so the stars on the flag went first when the remains exited the morgue tent. Everyone was always a little choked up, including me. We all stood at attention and saluted until the remains were put into the ambulance. Once the doors closed, we were told: "at ease." Then a police escort would lead the ambulance to the chief medical examiners on First Avenue and 28th Street.

It was especially gut-wrenching when we found other items, like yo-yos or toy cars, with the remains. After a while, things started to slow down, and I decided to take a break and go over to one of the ships providing free meals for the workers at Ground Zero.

"You look like you needed this." A volunteer approached me in the rest area, where I sat down to eat. She handed me a pre-paid ten-dollar phone card. With a confused look on my face, I swallowed my food and thanked her. She smiled at me and then continued walking down the line of first responders eating, giving out more phone cards to rescuers.

Once I finished eating, I took a slight detour before I went back to the temporary morgue. Along the way, I thanked the volunteers who fed me. They smiled, thanking me back. Those smiles were worth a million dollars when you were having a day like I was.

After walking down to the pier where the ship was docked, I finally got a chance to see the makeshift memorial. There were so many teddy bears, pictures, and notes, as well as mementos. I started reading some of the pleas from family members for their missing relatives, and I thought how lucky I was. The FDNY memorial was a little further down the wall. I recognized pictures of my buddies. I stared at them in silence.

My internal mood did not match this beautiful day. I stopped for a moment and looked at the quietly flowing Henry Hudson river.

A few minutes after, I checked my watch. It was time for me to head back. I saw the Hanoi Hilton, which was now off-limits and surrounded by NYPD officers. Apparently, after the first few days, people would take a breather in the bar, which was open, and...you know, free drinks. Well, that didn't go over too well with the mayor, so it was deemed off-limits.

I walked back inside the MASH tent that housed the temporary morgue and saw Mark sitting at the desk.

"How's things," I asked in a chipper, uplifting mood.

"Just fucking ducky, Rocky." He sighed.

"What's up?" I sensed the tension in his tone.

"More FDNY remains," Mark replied, throwing down his pen at the paper.

Instantaneously my chipper mood evaporated as reality slapped me across the face. I walked to the back of the tent, and as I opened the door, the priests were just finishing their prayer as a few firefighters stood by, teary-eyed. They picked up the remains draped in a US flag and proceeded outside to the waiting ambulance.

"Stars first!" someone yelled.

The firefighters turned the longboard around and proceeded outside with the stars first on the American flag.

As I walked over to the book where all the entries were made and initialed, I caught up on the entries that had been made while I was gone.

My tour at Ground Zero ended fifteen hours later. Our relief showed up, and I introduced them to the DMORT Team. As I was briefing them, it occurred to me that we no longer had to tell everyone to be wary of falling debris or the signals to evacuate. I left to catch a shuttle ambulance to the pier, then jumped into another ambulance.

After getting into the second ambulance, most of us decided to go home. Although at the beginning of the tour we had all agreed that we were going out to have a few beers at the end of it, by now we were exhausted, physically and mentally. I just wanted to go home.

"Hey, you guys, check out the crowd!" the driver up front spoke through the opening that separated the driver compartment from the patient compartment.

Citizens lined the street holding signs: "Thank You" and "We love FDNY/EMS." This time we were just too tired to open the back doors and wave. Instead, most of us closed our eyes and tried to sleep.

Today I didn't feel like a hero; today, I felt exhausted.

CHAPTER TWENTY

Reunion

As the weeks passed, I started to come to grips with grief. Some of us handled it better than others; everyone had their own way of sorting things out. Personally, I still had my doubts about myself. When am I going to crack up? I kept thinking. Sometimes I would look in the mirror and ask myself, are you okay? I started crying here and there; something would remind me of Ground Zero, and I'd excuse myself and hide in a corner somewhere and cry quietly for a minute.

It was close to five weeks after my last tour before I scheduled myself for a return to the WORLD TRADE CENTER. Before I got the chance to work, I was told to drop off a lieutenant down at Ground Zero to cover another lieutenant who was on his seventeenth hour. So off I went in a command car. I had no idea who the boss I would be dropping off was, but I picked him up at Battalion 52.

I kept quiet the whole time the boss was in the vehicle as I drove him down to Ground Zero. I had this feeling this guy, whoever he was, was not wrapped too tight. How shall I put it: "He was few cans short of a six-pack." I knew this when he started telling me that he'd seen UFO's landing at his Pennsylvania home. I just nodded my head and agreed. *Yeah, me too.*

After dropping him off, I saw Kevin, an EMT I worked with on and off during my career when my partner would be on vacation or off. He was drinking a soda near the opening of a condemned archway. There was no safe area around the worksite. He and another EMT, Barry, had helped me when we were in the academy. While Kevin and Barry were breezing through tests getting ninety-eights and me seventy-eights, they gave me acronyms to remember so I wouldn't get things mixed up. Stuff like "the difference between a strain and a sprain is: strain has a T in it, so you tear a muscle." After that, we became good friends. Without those two, I don't think I would be around telling this story.

When airline travel resumed at the end of 2001, I got away for a week with my wife, Jeanne. We traveled to Cancun, Mexico, like we did every year, except this trip was more somber. The Mexican people celebrated death a little differently than we do; it became more of a celebration, and a bottle of tequila was usually involved.

Back in 1300 A.D., the Aztecs built pyramids somewhat like the Egyptians, and even after all this time, some are still standing. Behind our hotel, you could occasionally visit a smaller pyramid that had been roped off as a historical landmark. Looking at the surrounding view, you could see why it was a special location that the Aztecs respected.

I caught myself one time standing alone with a drink in my hand, a Mariachi band playing in the background while looking off the cliff with one of those smaller pyramids behind me. I remembered Mike and thought of how he always said he loved Cancun. After watching the sunset slowly creep down behind the waters of the Gulf of Mexico, I said a quick prayer, then turned to rejoin my wife at the poolside.

I thought of the celebration of death—the Mexican philosophy—and noticed I had a medal around my neck of Saint Florian, like the ones that the chaplains always placed on FDNY remains at the WORLD TRADE CENTER. At the time, I kept a few in my pocket in case the chaplain wasn't around, and I would place it into the body bag that contained the remains myself. After working at the morgue detail a few times, I would come home and find I had one or two of the medals in my pocket and just leave them on the bedroom bureau. One day I decided to buy a simple sterling chain and attached one of the medals to it.

I turned around and headed back to the sacred place of the Aztecs. Once there, I took the necklace off and spoke to Mike, saying, "A little bit of you is back in one of your favorite places," and with that, I tossed the medal of Saint Florian and the chain into the sacred site. I also raised my glass to the sky and said, "We all miss you, Mike, and by the way, can you keep an eye out on my sorry ass for the remainder of the time I have left on this planet."

CLOSING CEREMONY, MAY 30TH, 2002.

It had been eight months since I first went down to the WORLD TRADE CENTER disaster site. There wasn't a whole lot more I could say other than we were all mentally burned out.

Jules Lisner from the Queens medical examiner's office walked over toward the makeshift morgue that was set to be dismantled in the next few hours. All body parts found from this day on would be going directly to the medical examiner's office on First Avenue.

"What the hell are you doing down here? I thought they closed up shop?" I asked Jules as I entered the tent.

"No, no, no, one more day," he replied.

The clergyman and Jules left in the Gator, but before they left, Jules came running back and asked,

"Rocky? Do you have a camera I can borrow?"

I did happen to have one, so I lent it to him and off they went into the pit, which was now transformed into a large construction site. I swear the only way you would think this was the site of some disaster was to look at all the memorials surrounding the site itself. Sixteen acres...that's what was destroyed.

For close to twelve hours, I looked at the site and compared it to the horrors I'd first witnessed. I looked at where the sixteen-story "mountains of steel" stood at one time. I took a walk to St. Paul's Church and once again asked God for guidance. *"Lord, take me where you want me to go, let me meet who you want me to meet, tell me what you want me to say, and keep me out of your way."*

Those memories haunt me every day, and the visions of death and destruction were far worse than any movie I ever saw. Nothing can come close to picking up and holding people's limbs torn away from their bodies or searching for names on your FDNY brothers tattered remains, hoping that somewhere you can come up with an ID.

I have been back to Ground Zero several times after that day. Each time i noticed less chaos and more order, if you will, to my surroundings.

EPILOGUE

Well, here we are some 20 years after September 11, 2001. Most if not all of us have been impacted one way or the other.

I retired in 2009, and to this day, I still go to the doctor and get checkups from being exposed to the elements that persisted during the most challenging part of my life, Ground Zero.

As you can tell, most stories that I recorded the way I did, ended after 9/11. I had several surgeries relating to on-the-job injuries and injuries I sustained during the tail end of my career.

I know there are still so many stories inside my bag. Some I cannot write about; others might've fallen through the proverbial cracks. At the end of the day, each of them reminds me of the people around me.

Some have been searching for answers, and some

have more questions now than they had some 20 years ago. All I know is that those who are still here, alive, carry the burden of life on each other's back. Life is not beautiful rainbows all the time. That's why having someone to share it with is special. It signifies hope when things aren't going the way you want them to.

I found myself writing portions of this book during the COVID-19 global pandemic. The disease ripped away more of my friends from me. But like a sunrise or a sunset, one knows another day is on the horizon soon, and that can make a world of difference. What is the past is done, what we all can do to make the future, it's up to us. After 60 years on this earth and with my mind full of memories, I find that's not all bad, just a little more complicated than I'd thought. (Actually, a LOT more complicated.)

I still say my prayers at night, believe it or not. I don't kneel at the bed anymore because I've had a few surgeries on my knees. I've kept busy and met beautiful people that I wouldn't trade anything for. I have done my best to keep in touch with all my coworkers and will continue to do so. It's what I do best.

The thing is... was it all worth it? "Would you do it all again?"

My answer is, "Yes."

Author's note

One hundred and two minutes elapsed between the first plane hitting the North Tower at 0846 hours and the collapse of the first and second WORLD TRADE CENTER towers. Even though the South Tower was hit second, it collapsed first, followed by the North Tower at 1029 hours.

The End

ABOUT THE AUTHOR

Steve C. Bialek

Steve was born and raised in Queens New York. His father was an electronics parts manufacturer, his factory made radio components that were in the Apollo and Gemini spacecrafts. His mother worked as a secretary in the offices of the World Trade Center. After obtaining the necessary knowledge he needed to heed his calling to help others, Steve joined the Emergency Medical services.

He continues to attend periodic doctor visits due to the illnesses and conditions he developed during his career and in Ground Zero.

Made in USA - Crawfordsville, IN
63222_9781737690313
01.18.2022 1008